ENCYCLOPAEDIA OF EMINENT THINKERS

VOLUME-XII: VEER SAVARKAR

Volumes by the same author

The Political Thought of ***Veer Savarkar***
The Political Thought of ***M.A. Jinnah***
The Political Thought of ***Mohammad Iqbal***
The Political Thought of ***K.B. Hedgewar***
The Political Thought of ***M.S. Golwalkar***
The Political Thought of ***Lokmanya Bal Gangadhar Tilak***
The Political Thought of ***Pandit Deendayal Upadhyaya***
The Political Thought of ***Gopal Krishna Gokhle***
The Political Thought of ***Maulana Abul Kalam Azad***
The Political Thought of ***Sir Syed Ahmed Khan***

About the Author

Dr. Jai Narain Sharma (*b.* 1951) is Professor and Chairman of the Department of Gandhian Studies, Panjab University, Chandigarh. He is also Hon. Director of Gandhi Bhawan; member of Board of Studies, Nagpur University, Nagpur and Mahatma Gandhi Kashi Vidyapith, Varanasi; member of Research Degree Committee of the Department of Political Science, H.P. University, Shimla: General Secretary of Indian Soviety of Gandhian Studies; and member on the Presidium of the Alliance for Sarvodaya. He regularly writes for leading newspapers, and has published more than hundred research papers in professional journals of repute. Dr. Sharma has many books to his credit including *"Gandhi's View of Political Power",* *"Economics of Defence: A Study of SAARC Countries", "Economic Thought of Mahatma Gandhi", "Human Resource Management", "Alternative Economics: Economics of Mahatma Gandhi and Globalisation", "Power, Politics and Corruption: A Gandhian Solution"* and *"Research Methodology: The Discipline and its Dimensions.*

ENCYCLOPAEDIA OF EMINENT THINKERS

VOLUME TWELVE

POLITICAL THOUGHT OF VEER SAVARKAR

Jai Narain Sharma
Professor & Chairman
Department of Gandhian Studies
Panjab University, Chandigarh

CONCEPT PUBLISHING COMPANY, NEW DELHI-110059

Cataloging in Publication Data—DK
Courtesy: D.K. Agencies (P) Ltd. <docinfo@dkagencies.com>

Encyclopaedia of eminent thinkers / K.S. Bharathi.
v. 11-15 ; cm. — (Gandhian studies and peace research series ; 11)
Vols. 11, 14-15 by Ashu Pasricha; v. 12-13 by Jai Narain Sharma.
Includes bibliographical references.
Includes indexes.
ISBN 13: 9788170226840 (set)
ISBN 10: 8170226848 (set)

1. Statesmen—India. 2. Political science—India. 3. India—Politics and government. I. Bharathi, K. S. (Kuduva Swamy), 1956- II. Pasricha, Ashu, 1967- III. Sharma, Jai Narain, 1951- IV. Series: Gandhian studies and peace research series ; 11.

DDC 954.035 22

ISBN -13: 978-81-7022-684-0 (Series)
ISBN -10: 81-7022-684-8 (Series)
ISBN -13: 978-81-8069-492-9 (Vol. XII)
ISBN -10: 81-8069-492-5 (Vol. XII)

First Published 2008

Published and Printed by
Ashok Kumar Mittal
Concept Publishing Company
A/15-16, Commercial Block, Mohan Garden
New Delhi-110059 (India)
Phones: 25351460, 25351794
Fax: 091-11-25357103
E-mail: publishing@conceptpub.com

DEDICATED
TO
THE SACRED MEMORY
OF
MY RESPECTED ELDER BROTHER
LATE DR. YOGESHWAR PRASAD SHARMA

PREFACE

Politics without history is rootless, and history without politics is fruitless. History supplies raw material to political developments. It provides us not only the record of genesis, of growth and decay of political institutions, but also their positive and negative aspects. It is the record of their cause and effect relationship too. To comprehend history properly, we must have an ontological concept strictly based on logic, and substantiated by the real world in which we live, act and experience. We may profit thus, in shaping the destiny of our times, both individually as well as collectively.

One really does not know whether providence has bestowed a special boon on this country. The innate vitality of our age-old society is extremely powerful. There is not a single period in its whole history when some exceptionally great personality, or the other, was not born to give everlasting credit to this nation. Great men have been born here, who not only freed the country from the evil forces but also dazzled the world at large with their extraordinary calibre in achieving the impossible in most adverse circumstances.

Modern Indian Political tradition is a fascinating, but complex field of study. Modern India has not produced a Manu or Kautilya, but many of Her contemporary leaders were creative individuals of a high order whose utterances gave expression to many important ideas. These were of great significance both in theoretical and practical politics. The student of modern Indian political thought is, therefore faced with fact that although there are no systematically worked-out theories of importance in his field of study, he cannot ignore the ideological implications of the views held by many statesmen, Savarkar is one of them.

Savarkar came on the political scene when India needed him most. He had to fight against odds as contradictory political theories held the field. He led the Hindu Mahasabha when to be a Hindu sanghatanist was not a paying concern and when all the avenues to power, pelf and popularity led elsewhere. To call oneself a Hindu was to be obstracized by one's own kith and kin for no other fault than of daring to love and defend the Hindu cause and Hindu honour. He advocated militarization when some leaders in all sincerity pleaded that India did not need an army, navy or air force and no nation in the world would invade her and if some armed nation did invade her they could be easily persuaded to fall back by soul force. Savarkar urged the Hindus to join the army, navy and air force in large numbers so that they might get the necessary training and experience in modern warfare. Savarkar always tried to reason with his opponents if their doubts and objections were genuine and his manner was persuasive. But when he found hypocrisy, imbecility and cowardice passing off as patriotism and generosity his attack grew virulent. He used satire and ridicule to expose the hollowness of such claims.

In fact, it is for the cool, calculating and balanced history to assess man's work with a cold impartiality and grade it great or otherwise. Feelings, passions and prejudices should not effect contemporary judgement, as has happened unexpectedly in the case of Savarkar, for they often result in misguided notions. Perhaps, history has made him liable for misunderstandings. Most biographers tend to divide his life into three water-tight compartments, namely, the period before his deportment to the Andaman, his life period in the Andaman and his life after the Andaman. They appreciate and admire the life of the man till his days in the Andamans, more for his literary genius than as a prophet of nationalism. The odds have played their part. Howsoever, the fact cannot fade that joint responsibility and real democracy only can lead to prosperity and security. The secular success lies not in being silent spectators, but in being willful contributors to the development of the country. Although violence is the last resort in a democratic set up, and indeed, it should be avoided as far as possible, but there are situations when only the remedy of the use of brute and ruthless force can work. For, moral homilies become ineffective. It is, therefore, the imperative responsibility to stand up and safeguard the cultural values of secularism and democracy. If we, as a nation, fail at this stage of catastrophe, India will lose its identity and the whole civilization that is claimed to last till eternity will witness an avoidable collapse. This is the relevance and message of Savarkar, in case we try to remove the chaff from the grain in his voluminous writings. Let the nation and its identity have the first and the last word.

Personal acknowledgements are no easy matters where so many have been kind. My special thanks are due to Professor S.L. Malhotra, Professor R.N. Pal, Professor N. Radhakrishnan, Dr. K.S. Bharathi, Dr. R.P. Dwivedi, Dr. A.D. Mishra, Professor B.R. Duggar, Dr. K.C. Agnihotri, Professor Raj Bir Singh Yadav, Professor M.L. Sharma, Dr. Meena Dutta, Dr. Ashu Pasricha and Dr. Rashmi Sharma. Beyond that I can make only an all embracing salute to the galaxy of the scholars whose works I have consulted.

I am also grateful to Shri Ashok Mittal my publisher for his consistent zeal in the printing and publication of this volume.

Chandigarh

JAI NARAIN SHARMA

Encyclopaedia of Eminent Thinkers Series

Vol. I. The Political Thought of **Mahatma Gandhi**/ *K.S. Bharti*
Vol. II. The Political Thought of **Nehru**/ *K.S. Bharti*
Vol. III. The Political Thought of **Rabindra Nath Tagore**/ *K.S. Bharti*
Vol. IV. The Political Thought of **Radhakrishnan**/ *K.S. Bharti*
Vol. V. The Political Thought of **Vinoba**/ *K.S. Bharti*
Vol. VI. The Political Thought of **Aurobindo**/ *K.S. Bharti*
Vol. VII. The Political Thought of **Jayaprakash Narayan**/ *K.S. Bharti*
Vol. VIII. The Political Thought of **Vivekananda**/ *K.S. Bharti*
Vol. IX. The Political Thought of **Ambedkar**/ *K.S. Bharti*
Vol. X. The Political Thought of **M.N. Roy**/ *K.S. Bharti*
Vol. XI. The Political Thought of **Dadabhai Naoroji**/ *Ashu Pasricha*
Vol. XII. The Political Thought of **Veer Savarkar**/ *Jai Narain Sharma*
Vol. XIII. The Political Thought of **M.A. Jinnah**/ *Jai Narain Sharma*
Vol. XIV. The Political Thought of **Tej Bahadur Sapru**/ *Ashu Pasricha*
Vol. XV. The Political Thought of **C. Rajagopalachari**/ *Ashu Pasricha*
Vol. XVI. The Political Thought of **Subhas Chandra Bose**/ *Ashu Pasricha*
Vol. XVII. The Political Thought of **Mohammad Iqbal**/ *Jai Narain Sharma*
Vol. XVIII. The Political Thought of **K.B. Hedgewar**/ *Jai Narain Sharma*
Vol. XIX. The Political Thought of **Bhagat Singh**/ *Ashu Pasricha*
Vol. XX. The Political Thought of **M.S. Golwalkar**/ *Jai Narain Sharma*

CONTENTS

CONTENTS

1

LIFE AND ACTIVITIES

After the unsuccessful first war of Independence of 1857 in the second part of the 19th century, the British imperialists strengthened their hold on India and hatched designs to keep the nation subjugated for all time to come. In politically fallen, socially degraded and financially ruined Hindustan, the eighteen eighties and nineties witnessed the darkest period in the history of our country. The first peep of the dawn in the form of reforms of 1909 was still to come. The dawn of 1919 was beyond the horizon. The political and economic discontent of the Indian people which had been gathering steadily, especially after 1870, almost threatened to reach an explosive point by 1883. The anti-popular measures of Lord Lytton's government seriously accentuated this discontent. These ill-starred measures of reaction, combined with Russian methods of police repression, brought India under Lord Lytton within measurable distance of a revolutionary outbreak, and it was only in time that A. O. Hume and his Indian advisers were inspired to intervene, resulting in the formation of the Indian National Congress in 1885. Hume made it quite clear that the Congress was designed as a safety valve for revolutionary discontent.

Siding with Hume, other historians also took the view: "The years just before the Congress were among the most dangerous since 1857. It was Hume, among English officials, who saw the impending disaster and tried to prevent it. He went to Simla in order to make clear to the authorities how almost desperate the situation became. It is probable his visit that made the new Viceroy, who was a brilliant man of affairs, realise the gravity of the situation and encouraged Hume to go on with the formation of the Congress. The time was fully ripe for this All-India movement. In place of an agrarian revolt, which would have sympathy and support of the educated classes, it gave the rising classes a national platform from which to create a New India."[1] It would be most appropriate to mention here that being in the government service till 1882, Hume received possession of the very voluminous secret police reports which revealed the growth of popular discontent and the spreading of underground conspiratorial organisation. The Ilbert Bill, the muzzled press, the Arms Act, the First Indian Councils Act of 1861, were all a part of quite a mournful period. At the same time, the struggle generated a spirit of keen revivalism. The effort had been to infuse a spirit of strength, dynamism, social solidarity and nationalistic fervour amongst the Hindus.[2]

In such an atmosphere surcharged with unfulfilled aspirations was born Vinayak Damodar Savarkar on Monday, 28 May 1883, at Bhagur, a village near Nasik—between the death of Marx and the birth of Mussolini. Seventy five days before Savarkar's birth, Karl Marx, the Prophet of the Proletariat, passed away unnoticed in a London corner and sixty two days after was born Benito Mussolini who later moulded the destiny of Italy.

Savarkar sprouted from the illustrious caste of Chitpavan Brahmins that produced Nanasahib of 1857-fame, Wasudeo Balwant and Lokamanya Tilak, all of whom strove to snatch the crown of Independence from the hands of the British. The Savarkars originally hailed from Konkan, a land symbolising the great feat of reclamation performed by Parshuram, who is a mighty mythological figure. During the declining days of Peshwa rule, the Savarkar's were an important family which had moved in and seen great events. They were Jagirdars of a small village, Rahuri, and enjoyed the honour of palanquin for their acknowledged eminence in Sanskrit scholarship. The blood, bones and brains of such ancestors carved out this epic figure of Indian revolution, Vinayak Savarkar, who declared a war for the liberation of Hindustan.

Savarkar was sent to the village school at the age of six. Soon he showed signs of his remarkable inborn genius. Much of his inspiration he derived from history and epics. His love of books and newspapers was so great that he read omnivorously, and any book or newspaper that he could lay his hand upon, he read from cover to cover. His studies were intense, exciting and prolonged. His depth and intelligence and the immense interest he took in human affairs can be judged from one incident. While reading the history of the Arabs, he asked his father about the first pages of their history. The first pages of the book were missing. Naturally, the father replied that they might have been torn off. What the boy, in fact, wanted to know was the antecedents of the Arabs. The range and loftiness of this idea touched the infinite universe. Savarkar depicted this idea in one of his latter day poems and concluded that the first pages of all history are always unknown! This is the curse of history, he added. Vinayak was hardly ten when well known newspapers from Poona accepted his poems, not knowing that the contributions came from a precocious lad. His insatiable thirst for knowledge, his excellent memory and the peculiar charm in his voice and gait impressed everyone and raised high hopes of his future.[3] It would be noteworthy to mention here that Vinayak's father, Damodarpant Savarkar, was a man of position and personality, and an admirer of Tilak. Vinayak's mother, Radhabai, was a pious lady. The two had three sons and one daughter. The first was Ganesh (born 15th June 1879), the second Vinayak, the third was a daughter named Mainabai (born 1886), and the fourth was Narayan (born 12th May 1888).

As a schoolboy at Poona and Nasik, Vinayak achieved distinction as a forceful speaker. He and his friends took a prominent part in promoting the cause of Swadeshi which had been resorted to as a weapon to fight against the Partition of Bengal. He preached boycott of foreign cloth and arranged for a huge bonfire of them. His biographer, Dhananjay Keer, says that the 'Poona bonfire of foreign clothes was the first in India.'[4] For having organised it, he was not only fined Rs. 10 by the Principal of his College, but was also expelled from it. He wrote some ballads on Tanaji and Baji Prabhu, the heroes of Maratha history, which were prescribed by the Government. Vinayak Savarkar also wrote brilliant prose, and won many prizes as a student. He organised a revolutionary part called Mitra Mela. Subsequently, its name was changed to Abhinava

Bharat.[5] In the year 1906 Vinayak Savarkar availed himself of a scholarship offered by the revolutionary Pandit Shyamji Krishna Varma and sailed for London. His main object was to have a look at the den of the British lion, to learn how to organise a revolution and carry on the struggle for the liberation of Hindustan by inculcating tenets of revolution into the brilliant brains of the cream of Indian students who went abroad for academic careers. Shyamji Varma was so much impressed by the whole hearted devotion of Savarkar to the cause of freedom that he joined the Abhinava Bharat and entrusted the management of his India House to the former. Savarkar made the India House the centre of his revolutionary activities. He brought Bhai Parmanand and Madam Cama into the revolutionary fold. Senapati Bapat and Madan Lal Dhingra also came under his influence and became revolutionaries. Madan Lal Dhingra became a devoted follower of Savarkar and on the first night of July 1909, shot and killed Sir Curzon Wyllie, an important official of the India House. The intended victim of Dhingra's revolutionary ardour was Lord Curzon who somehow escaped.[6]

The incident shook London to its marrow! As if some unsusal crowbar turned London upside down. India was the subject in every British cottage, in every paper in trains, in trams, at public squares and in markets, palaces and the British Parliament. Under the fiery eyes of the Britisher loyal Indians also trembled. Their holy tears overflowed. They assembled on July 5, 1909, at the Caxton famous Hall to condemn Dhingra at the meeting. Sir Mancherjee Bhownagari, Sir Aga Khan, S. N. Banerjee, B. C. Pal and Khaparde were loud in their denunciation. The meeting was attended by Maharaj Kumar of Couochbihar, Sir Dinshaw Petit, Fazalbhoy Karimbhoy and others. Sir Aga Khan, the chairman declared towards the end, "The meeting unanimously condemns Madan Lal Dhingra."

Just at this moment a defying voice from the thickly crowded hall roared, "No, not unanimously". The chairman angrily uttered: "Who says no?" Out came the reply, "I say no." The chairman pursued, "Your name please." Upon this some lost their patience and shouted "Pull him down, drive him out!" In a moment Sir Mancherjee Bhowangari jumped from the platform and ran in the direction of the voice. The challenging voice shot back, "It is me. My name is Savarkar."[7]

The British press attacked Savarkar as the inspirer of the murder of Wyllie. Newspapers now directly attacked Savarkar as the fountainhead of the tragedy. In India, his relations and colleagues were persecuted. Some lost their jobs; other their property. Harsh measures were adopted to crush the Indian students who were presented as incarnates of every possible evil under the sun. Students going to London were now required to produce certificates from local Government. And a Student Centre was opened by the India Office ostensibly to help the Indian students but actually to spy on their activities. Pandit Shyamji's Scholarship money for Spencer Lectureship was returned. The diplomas of the Pandit and Virendranath Chattopadhyaya were cancelled as a result of their writings and propaganda.

Though Savarkar passed the final examination of the Gray's Inn, the Benchers of the Inn refused to call Savarkar and Harnam Singh to the Bar. Thereupon Savarkar made an appeal to the authorities of the Gray's Inn. They appointed a Committee to inquire into the matter. Match as Savarkar was for the legal brains on the Committee and their cross-examination, nothing was proved against him though this Committee was aided by the Government of India.

At last the Committee of the Gray's Inn decided not to call him to the Bar unless he gave them in writing an undertaking that he would never participate in politics. Savarkar rejected their offer in toto! So did Harnam Singh. Getting the diploma was not his aim, but to free his country and make it great and powerful. This barrister was not meant for conducting petty cases and amass wealth. He was the nation's barrister. He was destined to study the case of his Motherland and put it before the world opinion as did Mazzini and Lenin. Hindustan knows how from the sunshine of his youth to the golden evening of his life, he remained a loyal barrister all along defending and fighting for the absolute political Independence of India, her integrity and her honour.

Savarkar was now on the verge of physical collapse. For the past four years he had worked with a phenomenal energy. Persecution reached its climax. A hell of wrath fell on him from all quarters. India House was closed down after the Curzon Wyllie incident. Savarkar requested Pandit Shyamji to relieve him from the work of the management of India House in March 1909. An angry mob surrounded the house of Bipin Chandra Pal with whom Sarvarkar was temporarily staying. Savarkar left the house next day and wandered in search of lodging. Shadowed as he was by the secret police, he could not secure any shelter and thus went to another place. From there he managed to publish the bold statement made by Madan Lal Dhingra before the court, much to the consternation of the police which tried its best to prevent its publication. The statement of Dhingra read:

"I admit, the other day, I attempted to shed English blood as an humble revenge for the inhuman hangings and deportations of patriotic Indian youths...I believe that a nation held in bondage with the help of foreign bayonets is in a perpetual state of war. Since open battle is rendered impossible to a disarmed race, I attacked by surprise; since guns were denied to me, I drew forth my pistol and fired. ... As a Hindu, I feel that a wrong done to my country is an insult to God ... The war of independence will continue between India and England so long as the English and Hindu races last (If this present unnatural relation does not cease)."[8]

Savarkar's activities in England were very strenuous and tiring. His health gave way and friends advised him to go to Paris for change and rest. All the while his lieutenants and revolutionary friends in India were active. Many of them were arrested, and some were sentenced to death while others were given long-term imprisonment and sent to Andamans for complicity in the Maniktola Bomb Case. Warrants for his arrest were issued from India. When news of the persecution of his friends and relatives in India reached him, he decided to surrender himself to the police and returned to London. There he was arrested by the police in 1910.

The warrant was granted by Bow Street Court, London, on February 22, 1910. The charges against Savarkar were:

1. Waging war or abetting the waging of war against His Majesty the King Emperor of India;

2. Conspiring to deprive His Majesty the King of the Sovereignty of British India or a part of it;
3. Procuring and distributing arms and abetting the murder of Jackson;
4. Procuring and distributing arms in London and waging war from London, and delivering seditious speeches in India from January to March 1906 and in London from 1908 to 1909.[9]

While he was being brought to India he jumped from the ship into the sea at Marseilles and escaped. He was however rearrested on French soil and brought by the same ship to India. Here he was tried by a special tribunal and sentenced to transportation for life. The Government of India instituted another case against him in which also be was given transportation for life. Two sentences of transportation one after another was unheard of judgement; it was a unique record in the political history of the world. Savarkar himself recorded:

"You are sentenced to fifty years transportation. The International Tribunal at Hague had also given judgement that England can not be constrained to hand you over to France, said Mr. X to me."

"Well then I have never depended on any hopes on that quarter. But can I have a copy of the judgement to look at."

"That does not rest with me, though I will try my best for you. Yet the fortitude you have shown in hearing the news that has wrung the heart of a stranger like me, does not make me think that you will wait for any help from an outsider like me." Said my interlocutor almost overwhelmed with feeling.

In the mean time a Sepoy brought to the Superintendent what looked like an iron plate. It was the badge, with the number marked on it, which a prisoner has to wear on his breast. The badge shows the date of his release. "What was my date? Am I ever to be free, or death alone was to be the date of my release? I cast my look on the badge and its number with mingled feelings of longing and despair, humour and curiosity. The year of my discharge was 1960. For a moment I did not take in the full significance of that writing. But, in a minute or two, it flashed upon my mind. I was sentenced in 1910 and I shall have my discharge in 1960."

The British Officer grimly observed, "No fear about it, the benign Government was sure to release you in the year 1960!

To him I replied in the same vein. "But Death is kinder. What if it lets me off much earlier?"[10]

Savarkar was given very hard job in the Cellular Jail. He was yoked to an oil-mill like a bullock. But he knew that each drop of oil that fell in the bucket would set aflame the hearts of all revolutionaries. It was this thought that helped and inspired him in the dark, difficult, agonizing solitary life in the Cellular Jail.[11]

Savarkar required terrific will power, strong determination and a passionate devotion to the cause to be able to face the deadly and maddening solitude of a solitary cell in Devil's Island. He did not complain, and suffered in silence. He even thought of committing suicide. But reason prevailed. For he wanted to die a hero in freedom's battle and not by committing suicide.

Savarkar endured all the sufferings, pain, agony, humiliation and sorrow. Few political prisoners of his stature ever suffered as much as this indomitable soldier. He had been put in bar fetters, cross-bar fetters and in standing handcuffs for long periods of time. He was made to eat foul food, live with rank criminals, denied human companionship and treated with utmost contempt. He drunk foul water, lived on stale bread, endured insults. The whole atmosphere was dreadful, devilish, dehumanizing and soulless. However, it was at Andaman that to secure the privileges of political prisoners for his comrades, this leader of thought, pioneer of a great cause, precursor of a revolution, prophet of a new order, maker of history, father of a political ideology and leader of a world famous revolutionary party, resolved to resort to agitation. In the eyes of the Government officials the name Savarkar had already become synonymous with sedition, and sedition had become synonymous with Savarkar.

It is not necessary to narrate Sarvarkar's life in the Andaman jail and the unbearable physical hardships he had to undergo as a revolutionary. However, it is worth recalling one event which sheds light on his great love for Hinduism. The usual practice in Indian jails having Hindu prisoners in majority was to appoint Muslim convicts as warders and havaldars. The latter were to use their petty authority for converting weak and suffering Hindus to Islam. Whenever Sarvarkar heard of the conversion of a Hindu convict to Islam for gaining some favours from the Muslim warders, he suffered great mental agony. One day the news reached him that a Hindu boy was on the verge of accepting Islam. When the Jail Superintendent came on his round, Savarkar lodged a complaint with him, and said that the Government should not permit such practices. To the Superintendent's remark that Hindus could as well try to convert Muslims, he retorted that the Hindus never sought to propagate their religion by offering material inducement. He further added that Hinduism looked upon all religions as at bottom being the same and therefore did not believe in proselytisation. This seems to have had some effect on the Superintendent and the boy was saved. The news created great stir in the jail and some prisoners began to carry on the propaganda and were able to reconvert some prisoners to Hinduism. Savarkar also impressed the truth upon the minds of his fellow-prisoners that it was foolish on their part to refuse to take food touched by Muslims.[12] All this infused a new spirit among the Hindu prisoners. It may be added that Savarkar did not despise Islam or hate the Muslims. He only abhorred the aggressive, unjust and wrong designs of the Muslim and Christian missionaries. He asked Hindus to shed inferiority complex and to organise themselves.

During the First World War, Savarkar made vigorous attempts to effect his release. It was only in 1921 that he and his elder brother who was also serving his term in the Andamans were brought to India for release.[13] The younger brother, Vinayak, was interned in his home district of Ratnagiri and was asked not to leave the limits of the district without the previous permission of the Government. He was further required to give an undertaking that he would not take part in any political activity for a period of five years. This restriction could be renewed for another period of five years. This internment and the restrictions placed on Savarkar's activities proved to be a blessing in disguise so far as the Hindu Mahasabha movement was concerned; they were responsible for turning the political revolution into a social revolution. Thenceforth Vinayak Damodar Savarkar devoted his great talents and indefatigable energy to the task of organising and consolidating the Hindus. It was largely as a result of his efforts from behind the scene that Ratnagiri Hindu Sabha was established with the object of organising and consolidating the Hindus into an organic whole with a view to enabling them to resist effectively any unjust aggression, and protecting their cultural, economic and religious rights. Through the Hindu Sabha Savarkar began to initiate the people of Ratnagiri into his new ideology. He did not believe in Gandhian non-violence; on the contrary, he held and taught that for the defence of their natural and national rights, the Hindu Sangathanists must use not only *lathis*, but, also machine guns and submarines if they could be secured and there was an opportunity to make use of them.

While interned at Ratanagiri, Savarkar carried an intense propaganda in favour of the removal of untouchability. He thought that one of the best ways to fight this demon was to establish mixed schools where the sons and daughters of the untouchables could receive instruction along with those of caste-Hindus. This roused the ‘anger of the orthodox people, but in the long run the forces of reform triumphed. The success of the mixed school greatly reduced the number of converts which the American Mission School could make, with the result that the Mission had to wind up its activities at Ratnagiri. The Ratnagiri Sabha reconverted many persons to the Hindu faith and also arranged for their marriages. Re-conversion was a war not only against the Hindu orthodoxy but also indirectly against the Christian and Muslim missionaries. The Christian missionaries complained to the District Magistrate that the activities of Savarkar were creating communal tension. Savarkar wrote to the Governor of Bombay explaining his stand, and convinced him of its justice. Because of such activities Savarkar began to be branded as a communalist. There is no doubt that in as much as they were calculated to awaken the Hindus to the prime necessity of organising themselves as a distinct community, they did encourage the communal spirit; but they were undertaken purely in self-defence. If Savarkar's activities were communal, those of the Khilafat workers were not less so.

Savarkar also supported the movement of admitting the untouchables to Hindu temples. He said: "He is not God who can be descerated.[14] Going further, he argued that those persons were a blot on humanity who felt polluted by the touch of a human being but gladly fondled cats and dogs. It is such people who are fallen and not the untouchables. Savarkar converted the Ganesh festival started by Tilak into a Pan-Hindu festival by allowing the untouchables to participate in it. In this way he could manage to take them inside the Vinoba Temple at Ratnagiri which is the most important temple in the whole district,. He also persuaded Seth Bhagoji Keer to build a magnificent temple known as *Patit Pavan Temple* wherein all Hindus irrespective of caste could go and worship the deity.

Savarkar decided to deliver another blow to Hindu orthodoxy. He organised a Pan-Hindu dinner known as Saha Bhojan in 1930. It was attended by *Brahmins, Banias, Chamars, Mahars* and *Bhangis*. Indeed, the spectacle of high and low caste Hindus dining together was grand and edifying. On this occasion Savarkar delivered a speech in which he observed as follows: 'From to-day I shall not believe in highness or lowness of caste. I shall not oppose the intermarriage between the highest and lowest castes. I shall eat with any Hindu irrespective of caste. I shall not believe in caste by birth or by profession, and henceforth I shall call myself a Hindu only, not Brahmin, Vaishya, etc."[15] He very appropriately said that the root of religion was not the dish or the stomach, but the heart, soul and the blood.

The aim of all the activities of Savarkar during this period of internment at Ratnagiri which extended to thirteen years was to mould the different castes of the Hindus into a classless Hindu society in which all Hindus would be by birth socially, economically and politically equal. Rational, nationalistic and revolutionary in outlook, his ideology was as deep rooted as it was far reaching, and stood for the prosperity and peace of the society, life, Hindustan, and ultimately universal welfare.

While Savarkar was living at Ratnagiri, many persons came to meet him. One of them was Hedgewar, the founder and organiser of the Rashtriya Swayamsevak Sangh. Before starting the movement Hedgewar had a long talk with Savarkar about its faith, form and organisation. It seems that he was greatly impressed by Savarkar's work on Hindutva which had been published near about that time. Gandhiji was another important visitor.

Savarkar was released from internment in May 1937, a little before Congress took office.[16] The story of his release is interesting. The Congress having declined to form the government in the Bombay Presidency, the Governor was anxious to form an interim ministry. Khan Bahadur Dhanjishaw Cooper and Jamnadas Mehta agreed to help the latter in forming a ministry on the condition that the Governor first released Savarkar. The Governor agreed and set Savarkar free. After release Savarkar did not join the Congress; he rather threw in his lot with the Tilakite Democratic Swaraj Party. The reason why he refused to join the Congress was that according to him it had departed from the democratic and national ideal by surrendering to the anti-national demands of the Muslims. Moreover, he disagreed with the Congress creed of non-violence. Though he too was a worshipper of the Goddess of Freedom, he was not willing to restrict himself to the use of non-violent means only. He favoured the employment of all available means. He once observed as follows: "The object of our worship is the Goddess of Freedom. The temple is one. Let the ways and means differ. The worshippers should not quarrel among themselves over the correctness of the means."[17] In the next place, he stood for the regeneration of the Hindus. The free and independent Indian State of his imagination was to be a *Hindu Rashtra;* the Hindus were to be the mainstay of its national life. His aim was to make the Hindus, who formed the majority on paper, conscious of the fact that they were the bedrock of the State. He urged them to start rifle classes, and to learn to handle at least the air gun.

The Hindu Mahasabha had no clear cut and inspiring programme at the time Savarkar was released from internment and joined it. The political events of that period had given rise to the vague awareness which had not till then found expression that the Congress policy of placating the ever growing demands of the Muslim League was full of dangerous consequences to the future of the Hindus. It became the mission of Savarkar to give pointed expression to this feeling and place before his co-religionists the ideology of *Hindu Rashtra* which first found full and vigorous expression in his Presidential address at the Calcutta session of the Mahasabha. He made a whirl-wind tour of the country, carrying his new message to the people everywhere he went, and made a tremendous impact on the minds of the people. He came to be recognised as the saviour of Hinduism.

One of the most important activities in which he was engaged in 1939 was the Civil Resistance movement carried on against the anti-Hindu policy of the Nizam of Hyderabad. The campaign was led by Savarkar and was conducted under the joint auspices of the Hindu Mahasabha and the Arya Samaj. According to Savarkar the most significant thing about the movement was its Pan-Hindu character. It was not only the Arya Samajists and the Sanatanists who participated in it but the whole Hindu brotherhood joined it. The sense of Hindudom or a common collective consciousness of Hinduism constitutes an integral part of the ideology of Hindu Rashtra. The Civil Resistance Movement which lasted for six months developed among the volunteers the feeling that Hindustan belonged to the Hindus. They uttered this slogan as they received *lathi* blows or whips of the cane. In the words of Savarkar, 'The fact that such a Hindu force consisting of fourteen to fifteen thousand civil resisters could be raised at the very first blare of the trumpet call by Hindu Sangathanist Party is a lesson for us and for all those who dare to treat our demands lightly.'[18] The second noteworthy feature of the Civil Resistance movement was that it was conducted against the wishes of the National Congress which called it 'communal' and therefore anti-national. This constituted a great departure from the past practice according to which the Hindus did not consider any movement to be 'national' which was not thus certified by the Congress. But this time the Hindu Sangathanist Party had an ideology of its own conception of what is really national or otherwise, interpreted in the light of reason that had freed itself from the blind and unquestioning subservience to any Papal bulls issued by the Congress Church and marched on to the rescue of their Hindu co-religionists...On that one single evening, for example, of the 'Nizam Nishedha Day' as well as the 'Hindu Nation Day' not less than a crore of Hindus were found gathered under the Hindu flag in the capital cities and towns throughout India in pursuance of the Mandate of the Hindu Sangathanist Party to back up the Hindu movement..[19]

In short, during the three years of his Presidentship of the Hindu Mahasabha, Savarkar did more to inculcate the feeling of Hindu Nationalism among the Hindus than could be achieved by his predecessors in a decade. Drawing the moral from the Hyderabad struggle Savarkar exhorted his audience as follows: 'Just think : if the Hindu electorate had voted for the Hindu Sangathanist representatives and thus had Hindu Mahasabha Ministries in Bombay, Madras and other parts, could they remain so callously indifferent to the oppression the Hindus had to undergo in Hyderabad? [20]

The second important event is the attitude adopted by Savarkar in the course of his talks with the Viceroy on the issue of the extent to which the Hindu Mahasabha could help in the Government's war effort. It reveals the extent to which it had diverged from the Congress standpoint. He told the Viceroy that he continued to be a revolutionary and complete independence of India was the goal he aimed at. Though he did not think that the Allies were fighting against the Germans out of altruistic motives, he was prepared to help the Government in the War Effort because it contributed towards the realisation of his objective, namely, militarization of the Hindus and industrialization of the country. At his instance the Working Committee of the Mahasabha passed a long resolution in November, 1939. It declared its conviction that no European nation involved in the war was guided solely by moral and altruistic ideas and that all of them were moved by considerations of national interest. Concerning the issue of Dominion Status *versus* Complete Independence, the Resolution laid it down that though the ultimate goal of the Mahasabha was absolute Independence of India, it was prepared to accept Dominion Status as the immediate first step towards that goal. It therefore asked the Government to introduce full responsible government at the Centre. In regard to the war effort, the Resolution declared that since the defence of India was the common concern of the Mahasabha and the Government, the former was willing to offer help in bringing the war to a successful issue. Its ultimate objective in asking the Hindus to join the army, navy and air force in as large a number as possible was to provide them an opportunity for getting military training. It was with a view to the general militarisation of the Hindus and the industrialisation of the country that the Mahasabha supported the expansion of the Viceroy's Council.

Savarkar was a champion of true democracy. He vigorously and successfully opposed all schemes of giving weightages and special representation in councils and services to minorities beyond all proportion to their numerical strength.

He fought for the integrity of India. When other leaders were willing to give the Muslim League 'so much that they would have no desire to ask for more' Savarkar stayed the hand of those who might have betrayed the Hindus and all that Jinnah could get was 'a truncated and moth-eaten' Pakistan.

Savarkar travelled through the length and breadth of India. Wherever he went he addressed mammoth gatherings. He was given the same welcome as is accorded to princes. Listening to him was an overwhelming experience.

Savarkar breathed his last on February 26, 1966. His loss was mourned by millions of Hindus. The President of the Indian Republic, the Prime Minister of India, and leaders of various political parties paid glowing tributes to the memory of this great revolutionary patriot and Hindu leader.

Savarkar will always be remembered by this grateful nation as a patriot who led the country through troubled times, and as a champion of true democracy. He united the Hindus under one flag and gave them an ideology that should inspire and guide them for generations to come.

REFERENCES

1. A.R. Desai, *Social Background of Indian Nationalism* (Bombay: Popular Prakashan), 1984, pp. 318-19.
2. V.P. Varma, *Modern Indian Political Thought* (Agra: Laxshmi Narayan Agarwal), 1974, p. 284.

3. Dhananjay Keer, *Veer Savarkar* (Bombay: Popular Prakashan), 1966, p. 2.
4. *Ibid.*, p. 19.
5. V.D. Savarkar, *My Transportation for Life* (Bombay: Sadbhakti), 1950.
6. *Ibid.*
7. Dhananjay Keer, *Veer Savarkar, op. cit.*, pp. 53-54.
8. V.D. Savarkar, *Swantantryaveer Savarkar: A Guide to Indian Revolutionary Movement* (Pune: Maharashtra Prantik Hindu Sabha), 1963.
9. V.D. Savarkar, *My Transportation for Life, op. cit.*, 1950.
10. *Ibid.*
11. M.K. Gandhi, Savarkar Brothers, *Young India*, 26-05-1920.
12. J.P. Suda, *Main Currents of Social and Political Thought in India*, Vol. III (Meerut: K. Nath), 1984, p. 439.
13. A.G Noorani, *Savarkar and Hindutva* (New Delhi: Leftword), 2002, p. 19.
14. V.D. Savarkar, *Hindutva* (Pune: Sadashiv), 1942, p. 71.
15. *Ibid.*
16. Jyoti Trehan, *Veer Savarkar Thought and Action of Vinayak Damodar Savarkar* (New Delhi: Deep and Deep), 1991, p. 31.
17. V.D. Savarkar, *Hindutva, op. cit.*
18. *Ibid.*
19. *Ibid.*
20. *Ibid.*

2

INTERPRETATION OF HISTORY

The general trend of the Histories, written, read and taught in schools and colleges has been one of eulogizing the foreigners and deprecating the Indian race, relying wholly on the biased records of the foreign historians and travellers. Attempts have been made by Savarkar to reconstruct and restate the history of India from the national point of view, using to the utmost all available native records of coins and inscriptions and covert allusions in the otherwise non-historical works. Slender though they may be but they still, sporadic and isolated, relating to this or that particular phase of Indian History. This section presents 'Six Glorious Epochs of Indian History' since the beginning of our recorded history i.e. from the days of Chandragupta Maurya to the end of the British dominance over India as advocated by Savarkar.[1]

According to modern historical research, the first phase of the dawn of our national life dates back almost from five to ten thousand years ago.[2] Like that of China, Babylon, Greece and other ancient nations, our ancient history, too, is clothed in the poetical garb of mythology. It is replete with anecdotes, folk lore, and deification of national heroes and heroines, and resorts to supernatural and symbolic description. Yet these ancient mythologies (*Puranas*) of ours are the pillars supporting the edifice of our ancient history.[3] Just as these extensive Puranic texts are a magnificent treasure of our ancient literature, our knowledge, our glorious deeds and our grandeur and wealth, in a similar way they are a vast store-house of the accounts of our past, desultory, chaotic, even at times ambiguous though it may be.

Our *Puranas*, however, are not 'history pure and unadulterated.'[4] They have not been included in Glorious Epochs by Savarkar. The main criterion of history is that the dates and places and descriptions of events referred to therein must necessarily bear the stamp of authenticity, and they should be corroborated, as far as possible, by foreign as well as indigenous evidence.

The account of our past which fairly stands this test begins approximately from the time of Lord Buddha. Hence many Indian and Western Orientalists have accepted the Buddhist period as the beginning of Indian history.[5] The incessant and indefatigable labours of these Orientalists may in future include some of the so-called 'Pauranic period' into the historical one if some new evidence were to come to light. Till then at least we have to regard the Buddhist period as the starting point of our history.

Again, in respect of establishing the authentic history of any nation beyond doubt, the convincing references in the contemporary literature of other nations are really invaluable. The ancient period of our history which can be supported by the now available, unimpeachable evidence in the historical records of countries other than India is the one which begins round about the times of Emperor Chandragupta Maurya. For, since the date of Alexander's so-called invasion of India, numerous references to events in India are to be found in the historical accounts of the Greek writers and the description of their travels by the Chinese travellers.

What should be the criterion for determining the Glorious Epoch? For that matter there are hundreds of glorious epochs in the history of our nation which stand the tests of poetic exuberance, music, prowess, affluence, the height of philosophy and depth of theology and many other criteria. But by the 'Glorious Epoch' Savarkar meant the one from the history of that warlike generation and—the brave leaders and successful warriors who inspire and lead it on to a war of liberation in order to free—their nation from the shackles of foreign domination, whenever it has the misfortune to fall a prey to such powerful fatal aggression and to grovel abjectly under it, and who ultimately drive away the enemy, making it an absolutely free and sovereign nation.[6] Every nation extols such epochs of the wars of independence which inflict crushing defeats on the enemy.

Great men should ordinarily be never compared with another. They are great in various ways. But if anybody tries to compare any such and extol the one to the derogation of the other, this hoax must be exposed and reputed completely. As long as Europe eulogizes Alexander alone as the great and tries to brow-beat his antagonists Emperor Chandragupta, by evading any reference to him, the Indian must need assert that if at all they are to be compared, Chandragupta was super Alexander in comparison with Alexander! Alexander ascended the throne of a strong nation, already won by his father and commanded an army that was also formed by King Philip. On the strength of this ancestral inheritance he bravely built up a strong Greek empire! But Chandragupta enjoyed no such heritage! He had not a single soldier under his command; besides he had been banished from his ancestral empire by his father! Only one man was at his side; it was Arya Chanakya! Under these circumstances he had to start a new! Yet he built up a mighty army, conquered the ancestral empire, and wiping out the Greek conquests under Alexander himself and under his general Seleucos Nicator, founded an Indian empire mightier even than that of Alexander himself!

The epoch which starts with the conquest of the Yavanas by Emperor Chandragupta, the Super-Shikandar is the First Glorious Epoch of Hindu victories over the aggressor.[7]

Pushyamitra who, with his armed might, completely exterminated the Greek intrusion which from the time of Alexander had often caused great harm to India, and who, therefore, rightly deserves the title, 'Yavan destroyer,' protected ably for 36 years not only the independence of India which he himself had won, but brought about the many sided development of his country and then died peacefully in 149 B.C.

In the sense in which Chandragupta's rout of the Greek pockets of influence in India is said to be the first glorious epoch of Hindu victories over aggressors, this total extinction of the Greeks in India at the hands of Yavan destroyer Pushyamitra becomes necessarily, the Second Glorious Epoch of Indian history.[8]

In the historical past, there lived and ruled good many Emperors in India, but there was hardly any as surprisingly popular as this Emperor Vikramaditya who exterminated the Saka Kushans so thoroughly that not a trace of any of them is found today. Even a foreigner, the Chinese traveller, Fa-hien (or Fa-hsien), who visited India in his reign, has paid a glowing tribute to the prosperity, happiness, wealth and contentment that had reached its height, throughout the whole of the Indian empire under the Guptas. Even today in the innumerable Indian villages the name of King Vikramaditya and his high sense, and administration of, justice is lovingly sung in folk tales and ballad. After having defended the powerful unitary Indian empire and developed it in every respect for more or less, thirty five years Samrat Vikramaditya died in 414 A.D. The epoch which began with the royal seal of Samrat Vikramaditya, the proud Victor of Saka-Kushans is the third Glorious Epoch of Indian History.[9]

Yashodharma of Malwa, defeated the Huns at Mandasore, about 528 A.D. and captured the powerful and cruel Hun leader Mihiragula. His regime may be said to be the fourth glorious epoch of Indian history.[10]

The foundation of the Maratha power as a powerful counter-blast to the might of the Islamic forces in India marks the efflorescence of the fifth glorious epoch of Indian history. Aggression against the enemy and not merely defence was the policy of the Maratha leaders. The latter took recourse also to guerilla warfare.[11]

India liberated from the domination of the British Empire and this great Indian republic is established. The practical politicians amongst the 'loyal Hindus' satisfied themselves with the thought that under the present circumstances whatever is obtained is not meagre. Though not the whole of Bharat, at least three-fourths of it is liberated in an undivided state. Quite a great boon indeed ! After about a thousand years a great new age of national importance has dawned in the history of the Hindus. As such the real strategy for the Hindus from the point of view of their own benefit and the greater glory of Hindutva is first to make the newly won Bharat wholly their own. The fragments that were left in the foreign hands could be attended to later on.

Immediately the British Union Jack which had been fluttering proudly over the Red Fort in Delhi over the heart of India as it were for the last hundred or a hundred and fifty years with overbearing imperial haughtiness, was pulled down and in its place was hoisted amidst tumultuous applause and the deafening cries of 'Hail, Indian Independence, all Hail to thee!' the tri-coloured flag of the independent, sovereign Government of India, with the 'Sudarshan" wheel imprinted on it.[12]

From the Western Seas came the British imperial power marching on us with the supercilious vanity that with the sword alone they would conquer empires and with the sword alone would they run them; and straightaway it climbed the Indian imperial throne of Delhi. But at last from the very same throne of Delhi was it dragged down, its vaunting sword being cut to pieces ! To the shores of the very same Western Seas it was driven back and was ultimately submerged into the very same Western Seas! The last defeated British soldier, we saw with our own eyes going back to the same Western Seas with his head hung down and back towards us.

Thus of all the foreign aggressions over India that took place during the last two thousand years, the greatest and mightiest one —the sixth in order—that of the British was in the end utterly defeated by India and its political domination crushed to pieces.

Thus disappeared the mighty English empire. And when it did disappear, it did so, so very suddenly and speedily, so very completely, that the transfer of the empire instead of appearing to be the transfer of power appeared to be a change of dream. Till but yesterday not a straw moved in India without express orders from the English! But today, not an English Officer is to be found in India.

This victory over the English which deserves the Commemoration by A Horse-Sacrifice is the sixth of the glorious Hindu victories over foreign aggressors.[13]

Savarkar's interpretation of Indian history is parked by an intense and passionate glorification of vedic Hinduism. Not only is he opposed to the cult of pacifism, forgiveness and generosity popularized by Buddhism but he even asserts that "the Buddhists often betrayed, the cause of Indian independence and Indian empire."[14] He has eloquently praised the commentator Medhatithi on the Manu Smriti and Vidyatanya for the former's support to Hindu expansion and the latter's patronage of liberalism.[15] Shivaji is extolled for having established a Hindu independent state and for having "himself reconverted" Nimbalkar and Palkar who had been forcibly converted to Islam.[16] He is trenchant in the denunciation of the misplaced generosity of the Hindus against several of the Muslim invaders who resorted to barbarian tactics. Even Akbar has to face the bitter wrath of Savarkar. "This comparative greatness history can concede to him, and we do not hesitate to call him as great as he really was, but with all that greatness he was, from our Hindu point of view, foreign, belonging to another religion and mean minded and as such he should be decried by us, Hindus."[17]

In his Hindu-Pad-Padshahi Savarkar has given a nationalistic interpretation of the rise of the Maratha power.[18] In his book he reveals that the successful assumption by the Marathas of political power was a natural counterpoise to the policy of conquest, aggression, hatred and fanatical intolerance of the Moslems. According to him the Marathas were imbued with a loftier idealism than Harshavardhan and Pulakesin.[19] He has tried to show that the Maratha leaders in their conception of political authority, were imbued with the ideals of *Swadharma* and *Swaraj*. He also finds democratic elements in the Maratha polity.

Savarkar was one of the earliest exponents of the view that the so-called Sepoy Mutiny of 1857 was, really, the first war of Indian independence. He has tremendous admiration for the heroes of that epochal struggle. The struggle of 1857 having its operative theatre in farflung areas from Peshawar to Calcutta was activated by the noble and inspired concepts of "*Swadharma* and *Swaraj*." It is minimizing its great and phenomenal characters to interpret it as a minor mutiny. The fear of "greased cartridges" and the annexation of Oudh were only its accidental and temporary causes. The real motivating force of the great struggle was the wrath at the destruction of God-given liberty and the imposition of political slavery. It was this vital motive to save the religion and the motherland that drew blessings both from temples and mosques.[20] In support of his thesis Savarkar quotes from two authorities:

1. "It was not alone the sepoy who rose in revolt; it was not by any means a merely military mutiny. It was a combination of military grievance, national hatred, and religious fanaticism against the English occupation of India. The Meerut Sepoys found, in a moment, a leader, a flag, and a cause, and the mutiny was transformed into a revolutionary war. When they reached the Jumna glittering in the morning light, they had all unconsciously seized one of the great critical Moments of history, and converted a military mutiny into a national and religious war."[21]
2. "The movement, now, assumed a more important aspect. It became the rebellion of a whole people incited to outrage by resentment for imaginary wrongs and sustained in their delusions by hatred and fanaticism."[22]

Nana Sahib, in Savarkar's view, wanted to wage a united fight against the Britishers and "to make India free, and by removing internecine warfare, establish the rule of the United States of India."[23] But philosophizing on the final failure of the 1857, Independence movement, Savarkar does acknowledge that the constructive philosophy behind the struggle was not well laid out.[24] Had an attractive new ideal been set out, perhaps the traitors also would have turned into patriots.

REFERENCES

1. V.D. Savarkar, *Six Glorious Epochs of Indian History* (New Delhi: Rajdhani Granthagar), 1971.
2. R.C. Majumdar, H.C. Rai Choudhri and Kali Kumar Dutta, *An Advanced History of India*, 1950, p. 24.
3. Jawala Prasad Singhal, *The Story of Pre-historic Nations,* 1963, p. 11.
4. *Ibid.*
5. B.G. Gokhale, *Samudra Gupta Life: Life and Times*, 1962, p. 127.
6. V.D. Savarkar, *Six Glorious Epochs of Indian History, op. cit.*, p. 3.
7. *Ibid.*, p. 59.
8. *Ibid.*, p. 87.
9. *Ibid.*, p. 111.

10. *Ibid*., p. 126.
11. *Ibid*., pp. 452-53.
12. *Ibid*., p. 474.
13. *Ibid*., p. 475.
14. *Ibid*., p. 86.
15. *Ibid*., p. 202.
16. *Ibid*., p. 203.
17. *Ibid*., p. 402.
18. V.D. Savarkar, *Hindu-Pad-Padshahi* (Pune: Kalker), 1925.
19. *Ibid.*
20. V.D. Savarkar, *The Indian War of Independence* (New Delhi: Phoenix), 1947, pp. 6-7.
21. Justin McCarthy, *History of Our Times*, Vol. II
22. Charles Bell, *Indian Mutiny*, Vol. I, p. 644.
23. V.D. Savarkar, *The Indian War of Independence, op. cit*., p. 75.
24. *Ibid*., p. 542.

3

HINDUTVA

The ideal and ideology which Savarkar laid down and propagated is called the Hindu Sanghatan ideology or Hindu nationalism or Savarkarism. Although a natural development, an outgrowth and a manifestation of the various views and tenets upheld by several Hindu nationalists jointly, severally or individually, the ideology is put into a form and finally formulated and codified into an integrated doctrine of social and political outlook on life by Savarkar.

There were great Hindu leaders of Thought before Savarkar or existed even in his day, but none of them advocated all the principles or singly fought for them. They were stone-masons to this ideology, but the sculptor was Savarkar. In modern times Vivekananda, Tilak, Lajpat Rai and Hardayal were looked upon as great Hindu leaders of Thought, who spoke and wrote about Hindu thought. Vivekananda was a great philosopher, who devoted his lifetime and great talents to the unfolding of the Hindu philosophy and propagated it without political bias or a desire to win worldly gain to Mother India. Nevertheless, he was of the opinion that a nation in India must be a union of the those whose hearts beat to the same spiritual tune.[1] His ideal for India was 'an Islamic body with a Vedantic heart.[2]

Conscious of the separatist tendencies of the Muslims, Lajpat Rai, a staunch Hindu leader, held that Hindus were a nation in themselves because they represented a type of civilization their own. Hardayal wrote in the *Pratap* of Lahore in 1925: "I declare that the future of the Hindu race, of Hindustan and the Punjab, rests on these four pillars—(1) Hindu Sanghatan, (2) Hindu Raj,

(3) Shuddhi of Moslems; and (4) Conquest and Shuddhi of Afghanistan and the Frontiers. So long as the Hindu Nation does not accomplish these four things, the safety of our children and great grandchildren will be ever in danger, and the safety of the Hindu race will be impossible."[3] Tilak, a representative leader of Hindu Thought, had neither the time nor an opportunity to apply his mind to the geographical nationalism of his day. The only seer, who was conscious of this ideology in some way, was Dayananda. But unlike Savarkar, he perhaps held that there was no knowledge beyond the *Vedas;* besides, Dayananda was more a social than a political force.

Bhai Parmananda was a strong advocate of the concept of the Hindu Nation, Swami Shraddhananda and Bhai Parmananda were kin to Lajpat Rai just as Hardayal was kith to Savarkar; but none was kin to Savarkar. Before Savarkar there were promoters of Hindu solidarity and advocates of the removal of untouchability in Maharashtra and in other provinces too. As saviours of Hindustan they did their work in their own way, according to the demands of their times and needs.

There were champions of Hindu nationalism amongst the contemporaries of Savarkar. But the ideas of the social reform of Savarkar's predecessors and the politics of his contemporaries found a rare combination in Savarkar. Savarkar held definite thoughts on the rejuvenation of the Hindus. His approach to the Hindu-Muslim problem, the doctrine of absolute non-violence in thought, word and deed, and the foreign policy distinguished him from all other leaders; and his radical views about social regeneration and revolution, political concepts and precepts of a nation, economic policy, problem of the national script and *lingua franca,* and his ideas about a World Commonwealth form the Hindu Manifesto of a social and political system. It is laid down, in an outspoken, concise and virile form, sustaining the Hindus' struggle for existence and enabling them to contribute to the peace and prosperity of the world. No wonder then that, Savarkar's monumental work entitled, 'Hindutva' was acclaimed by Swami Shraddhananda as a message given at the dawn of a new age; and Savarkar's famous presidential speech at Ahmedabad giving the fundamental principles of the Hindu nationalism was hailed by Bhai Parmananda as the Bible of Hindu Sanghatan.[4]

What is Hindutva?

The word Hindu is the heart of that ideology, and Hindustan its geographical centre.

According to Savarkar, "every person is a Hindu who regards and owns this Bharat Bhoomi—this land from the Indus to the seas, as his Fatherland and Holyland—the land of origin of his religion and the cradle of his faith."[5] Therefore it follows that the followers of Vedism, Jainism, Buddhism, Sikhism and all Hill tribes are all Hindus. Around this life-centre moves Hindutva which Savarkar defines as not Wily the spiritual or religious history of our people, but the history in full pervasion. Hinduism is only a derivative, a fraction, a part of Hindutva. Hindutva is not, he observes, particularly theocratic, a religious dogma or a creed. It embraces all the departments of thought and activity of the whole being of the Hindu race. Forty centuries, if not more, he states, had been at work to mould it as it is. Prophets and poets, lawyers and lawgivers, heroes and historians, have thought, lived, fought and died just to have it spelled thus.

There are three fundamental criteria for being included under Hindutva or for being a Hindu. First, the territorial bond of *rashtra* is a primary requirement. A Hindu is one who feels attachment for the geographical region extending from the Sindhu river to the Brahmaputra and from the Himalayas to the Cape Comorin. Secondly, the racial or blood bond or the *jati*. A Hindu is one who inherits the blood of the race "whose first and discernible source could be traced to the Himalayan altitudes of the Vedic Saptasindhu". This is no preaching of historical existence, the Hindu have developed a physiognomy and racial features that are in some respects different from those of the Germans, Chinese or Ethiopians. Savarkar writes:

"No people in the world can more justly claim to get recognized as a racial unit than the Hindus and perhaps the Jews. A Hindu marrying a Moslem may lose his caste but not his Hindutva. A Hindu believing in any theoretical or philosophical or social system, orthodox or heterodox, provided it is unquestionably indigenous and founded by a Hindu, may lose his sect but not his Hindutva—his Hinduness—because the most important essential which determines it is the inheritance of the Hindu blood. Therefore, all those who love the land that stretches from Sindhu to Sindhu, from Indus to Seas, as their fatherland and consequently claim to inherit the blood of the race that has evolved, by incorporation and adaptation, from the ancient Saptasindhu, can be said to possess two of the most essential requisites of Hindutva".[6]

The third criterion of being a Hindu is culture or Sanskriti. A Hindu is one who feels pride in the Hindu culture and civilization represented in common historical memories of achievements and failures, in common artistic, literary and juristic creations and in common rituals or festivals or other media of collective expression. Thus, Moslems and Christians who have been converts from Hinduism cannot claim to be Hindus because they do not subscribe to Hindu culture. Thus, the three bonds of Hindutva are *rashtra, jati* and *Sanskriti*. According to Savarkar, the concept of Hindutva is broader and more comprehensive than Hinduism. Hinduism has a religious significance and connotes the theology and ritualism of the Hindus. Hindutva does comprehend within it this religious bond of Hinduism but goes beyond. Within Hindutva are included the social, moral, political and economic aspects as well. Hindutva cannotes the notion of an organic socio-political body knit together by the three bonds of territorial belongingness, blood or birth and culture.

Savarkar firmly believes in the doctrine of Hindutva or Hindu solidarity. In a competitive world full of tensions and struggles for power, the solidification of strength is the sole means of survival. Hindutva, as interpreted by Savarkar, is not only a concept of organic socio-political unity, it comprehends also the essential elements of nationalism. It is a programme for action. All the barriers that separate the Hindus have to be demolished. Savarkar favoured inter-marriages between all sections of Hindus. He included the Jains, the Sikhs, the Arya Samajists and the Brahmo Samajists also amongst Hindus. He said, "consolidate and strengthen Hindu nationality; not to give wanton offence to any of our non-Hindu compatriots, in fact to any one in the world, but in just and urgent self-defence of our race and land; to render it impossible for others to betray her or to subject her to unprovoked attacks by any of those 'Panisms' that are struggling forth from continent to continent!"[7]. This movement is called Hindu Sanghatan, which means an organization for the solidarity and strength of the Hindu Nation.

A nation is a group of mankind which is bound together with some or all of these common ties such as common religion and culture, common history and traditions, common literature, and consciousness of common rights and wrongs, occupying a territory geographical unity, and aspiring to form a political unit. When a nation realizes this ambition, it becomes a State. A nation may be without a State. A State is a governmental unit and it may have more nationalities than one under its rule. By 'nationality', C. B. Fawcett, the author of *Frontiers—A Study in Political Geography*, understands the group of qualities which characterize the people of any one nation. French nationality, he says, is that group of qualities which distinguishes the French from other European people.[8]

The principal elements instrumental in the formation of a nation are a common past, a common tradition and a will to live together. Renan defines a nation as a social group whose solidarity has been established by the sentiment of the sacrifices made in the past and of those it is still ready to make in the future. In his essay on nationality he observes that "a nation is a living soul, a spiritual principle. One is the common possession of a rich heritage of memories; the other is actual consent, the desire to live together, the will to preserve worthily the undivided inheritance which has been handed down." According to Harold J. Laski, it (nationality) implies a sense of special unity which marks off those who share in it from the rest of mankind. "That unit is the outcome of common history, of victories won and traditions created by a corporate effort. There grows up, a sense of kinship which binds men into oneness. They recognise their likeness, and emphasize their difference from other men."[9] Holland Rose writes that the nationality is at its height a union of hearts once made, never unmade a spiritual conception unconquerable, indestructible."[10] "In reality," observes Garner, "a nation is not a portion of society politically organised, that is, it is not a State, but in its perfect form it is a portion of a society definitely separated from the rest of the world by natural geographical boundaries, the inhabitants of which have a common civilization, common customs, traits of character and traditions," Israel Zangwill in his Principle of Nationalities discusses some of the factors that constitute a nation, viz. unity of religion, unity of language, possession of common traditions of suffering and of joy. By tradition he means songs, legends, stories attached to heroes, etc. "A nationality," states Durkheim, the Belgian Sociologist, with admirable brevity, "is a group of which the members, for racial or merely historic reasons, wish to live under the same laws and form a State."[11] G.P. Gooch, an eminent historian, in his Nationalism dealing with some factors that constitute a nation, observes: "But the strongest of all is the identity of political antecedents; the possession of a national history and consequent community of recollections; collective pride and humiliation, pleasures and regret, connected with the same incidents in the past."[12]

Hindu Nation

Savarkar's stand was that in Hindustan, the Hindus were a nation, and other people were communities and numerically, therefore, minorities. Savarkar observes: "The ancient and modern history of the Hindus is common. They have friends and enemies in common. They have faced common dangers and won victories in common. One in national despair and one in national hope, the Hindus by an admirable process through assimilation, elimination and consolidation are welded together during the aeons of a common life and common habitat."[13] Above all, the Hindus are bound together, continued Savarkar, by the dearest ties, most sacred and most enduring bonds of a common Fatherland and common Holyland. Verily the Hindus, stated Savarkar, as a people differ most markedly from any other people in the world than they differ among themselves. All tests whatever of a common country, race, religion, language that go to entitle a people to form a nation, entitle the Hindus with a greater emphasis to that claim.

According to Savarkar, the festivals and cultural forms of the Hindus are common. The *Vedic rishis* are their common pride, their Grammarians Panini and Patanjali, their poets Bhavabhuti and Kalidas, their heroes Ram and Krishna, Shivaji and Pratap, Guru Govind and Banda are a source of common inspiration. Like their ancient and sacred language the Sanskrit, their scripts also are fashioned on the same basis and the *Nagari* script has been the common vehicle of the sacred writings since centuries in the past.

India is dear to us, further observed Savarkar, because it has been and is the home of our Hindu race, the land which has been the cradle of our prophets and heroes, and Gods and Godmen. Otherwise, he went on, land for land, there may be many a country, as rich in gold and silver on the face of the earth. "River for river," asserted Savarkar, "the Mississippi is nearly as good as the Ganga and its waters are not altogether bitter. The stones, trees, and greens in Hindustan are just as good or bad stones and trees and greens of the respective species elsewhere. Hindustan is a Fatherland and Holyland to us not because it is a land entirely unlike any other land in the world, but because it is associated with our history and has been the home of our forefathers wherein our mothers gave us the first stickle at their breast and our fathers cradled it on their knees from generation to generation."[14]

According to the believers in Indian nationalism, a nation meant peoples living in its common land. Whoever came to India—the Arabs, the Jews, the Russians, the Germans, the Portuguese, the Greeks—formed a nation together with the Hindus, because these new-comers also lived in India. "Congress committed the serious mistake," stated Savarkar, "at its very start of overlooking this fundamental social and political principle that in the formation of nations, religious, racial, cultural and historical affinities count immensely more than their territorial unity."[15] What they called Indian Nation, Savarkar called the Indian State, because he believed that the Hindus could form a State with other minorities.

Savarkar found nothing objectionable in the ideal of Indian Nationalism. It was, in fact, said he, a noble ideal suited to the Hindu mentality with its synthetic trend, always prone to philosophy with a universal urge. It is also true, he believed, that the ideal of politics itself ought to be a human state, all mankind for its citizens and the earth for its Motherland. But is territorial unity the only constituent of a common nationality? "Not territorial unity", he replied, "but the religious, racial and cultural unity is what counts most in the formation of a national unit". The idea of territorial nationality alone was envisaged by the Congressites, who in general preferred to be totally ignorant of Muslim history, theology and political trend of mind.

Savarkar observed : "Moslems in general, and the Indian Moslems in particular, have not yet grown out of the historical stage, of intense religiosity and the theological concepts of State. Their theological politics divide the human world into two groups only—the Moslem land and the enemy land. All lands which are either inhabited entirely by the Moslems or ruled over by the Moslems are Moslem lands. To any other land no faithful Moslem is allowed to bear any loyalty."[16] Their Holyland is far off in Arabia. Their mythology and godmen, ideas and heroes are not the children of this soil. Consequently, their names and their outlook small of foreign origin. Their love is divided. Their love for India as their motherland is there but it is a handmaid to their love for their Holyland outside India. "The territorial patriots wanted the Hindus to cease to be Hindus, at least as a national and political unit. Some of them actually gloried in disowning themselves as Hindus. But the Moslems remained Moslems first and Moslems last and Indians never"[17] said Savarkar.

After the fiasco of the Khilafat, the Muslims exploded the Congress myth of territorial nationalism by migrating to Moslem lands. Greece, Palestine and even Hungary and Poland have thousands of Moslems amongst their nationals. China has crores of Moslems. Yet the country of the Poles continues to be Poland, of the Grecians Greece. There the Moslems did not dare to distort them, but are quite content to distinguish themselves as Polish Moslems, Grecian Moslems or Chinese Moslems. But the Indian Moslems never identified their aspirations with the national aspirations of Hindustan.

Gokhale had realised that the "seventy millions of Mohammedans were more or less hostile to the national aspirations,"[18] and warned Sarojini Naidu that the Hindu-Moslem unity would never come in their lifetime.[19] Pherozeshah Mehta had warned the British Government against the unjust Muslim claims. Lala Lajpat Rai too had fully realized the danger of the separatist tendencies of the Muslims[20] and Dr. Annie Besant had foretold in her *Future of Indian Politics* as early as 1922 that the primary allegiance of Muslims was to Islamic countries, not to our Motherland, and warned in her memorable words: "In thinking of an Independent India, the menace of Muslim rule has to be considered."[21] As late as 1941, B.R. Ambedkar expressed the same kind of grave doubt about Moslem allegiance to India when he said, "Islam can never allow a true Muslim to adopt India as his Motherland and regard a Hindu as his kith and kin."[22]

In Savarkar's view, so far as the Hindus are concerned, there can be no distinction or conflict in the least between their communal and national duties, as the best interest of Hindudom are simply identified with the best interests of Hindustan as a whole. The truer a Hindu is to himself as a Hindu, he must inevitably grow a truer national as well. The Hindus are the bedrock on which the Indian Independent State could be built. He asserted: "A Hindu patriot worth the name can't but be an Indian patriot as well. To the Hindus, Hindustan being the Fatherland and Holyland, the love they bear to Hindustan is boundless. That is why they predominate in the national struggle that is going on for the overthrow of the British yoke. Even the buried bones in the Andamans would assert this fact."[23] Further: "We Hindus must have a country of our own in the solar system and must continue to flourish there as Hindus' descendants of a mighty people."[24] Hence their solidarity, unity and strength should be kept intact. So *shuddhi* for him has not only a religious, but also a political, national and a secular meaning. If the population of the Hindus dwindles and the strength of the other faiths out numbers them, there would be a serious threat to the building of peace and prosperity, nay, to the very existence of Hindustan.

Savarkar believed in the resurrection of the Hindus, who have stood by the graves of empires and civilizations that prospered in other parts of the world. He believed that there was some such virility and staying power inherent in the Hindu race as could find few parallels in the annals of the world. Therefore, he observed that amidst the terrible struggle for existence, which was incessantly going on in the creation, survival of the fittest was the rule. The Hindus survived the national cataclysms because they were found the fittest to survive.

Savarkar propounded some of the basic tenets and aspects of the Hindu movement. He proclaimed:

1. "Every person is a Hindu who regards and owns this land of Bharatvarsha, from the Indus to Seas, as his Fatherland as well as his Holyland, that is, the land of the origin of his religion, the cradle of his faith." The followers, therefore of Vaidicism, Sanatanism, Jainism, Buddhism, Lingaitism, Sikhism, the Arya Samaji, the Brahma-Samaj, the Devasamaj, the Prorthana Samaji and such other religions of Indian origin are Hindus and constitute Hindudom, that is, the Hindu people as a whole. Consequently, the so-called aboriginal or hill tribes also are Hindus because India is their Fatherland as well as their Holy land of whatever form of religion or worship they follow.[25]

   A nation is a group of people bound together by some or all of these common ties such as common religion and culture, common history and traditions, common literature and consciousness of common rights and wrongs, occupying a territory of geographical unity, and aspiring to form a political unit.
2. The word Hindu is not of a foreign origin nor it is connected with the advent of the Moslems in India, as was erroneously suspected for a time under the mischievous influence of some alien scribes. Our land and our people were at times called Sapta Sindhus or Sindhus even by our Vedic Rights.
3. In expounding the ideology of the Hindu movement it is absolutely necessary to have a correct grasp of the meaning attached to the three terms—Hinduism, Hindutva and Hindudom. Hindutva is not identical with what is

vaguely indicated by the term Hinduism.[26] The third word 'Hindudom' means the Hindu people spoken of collectively. It is a collective name for the Hindu world, just as Islam denotes the Moslem world or Christiandom denotes the Christian world.

4. "We Hindus, inspite of thousand and one differences within our fold or bound by such religious, cultural, historical, racial, linguistic and other affinities in common as to stand out as a definitely homogeneous people as soon as we are placed in contrast with any other non-Hindu people, say the English or Japanese or even the Indian Moslems. That is the reason why today we the Hindus from Kashmir to Madras and Sindh to Assam will be a Nation by ourselves while the Indian Moslems are on the whole more inclined to identify themselves and their interests with Moslems outside India than Hindus who lived next door, like the Jews in Germany."[27]

5. Swarajya to the Hindus must mean only that 'Rajya' in which their 'Swatva', their 'Hindutva' can assert itself without being overloaded by any non-Hindu people, whether they be Indian Territories or extra territorials ... all that an Indian National State can mean is that the Moslem minority in India will have the right to be treated as equal citizens, enjoying equal protection and civic rights in proportion to their population. The Hindu majority will not encroach on the legitimate rights of any non-Hindu minority. But in no case can the Hindu majority resign its right which as a majority it is entitled to exercise under any democratic and legitimate constitution. The Moslem minority in particular has not obliged the Hindus by remaining in minority and therefore, they must remain satisfied with the status they occupy and with the legitimate share of civic and political rights that is their proportionate due. It would be simply preposterous to endow the Moslem minority with the right of exercising a practical veto on the legitimate rights and privileges of the majority and call it a '*Swarajya*.'

6. Consequently, the name 'Hindustan' must continue to be the appellation of our country.
7. As regards the Pan-Hindu Flag, the *Gerua* (Saffron) Flag shall be the Flag of the Hindu Nation. With its OM, the Swastik and the Sword, it appeals to sentiments cherished by our race ever since the Vedic days. It must be emphasised in this connection that all those Hindu flags other than this which are current amongst the Hindus as the colours of the different constituents which go to form our Pan-Hindu brotherhood such as the Sanatanists, the Sikhs, the Jains, the Aryans etc. will be respected by every Hindu as his own, in as much as they are but different manifestations of the common Pan-Hindu spirit. Nor should it be supposed that the Hindu Flag implies any inherent antagonism to the several colours of our non-Hindu countrymen. The Moslems are welcome to have their own religious colours to represent their own community.
8. The Sanskrit shall be our 'Devabhasha', our sacred language and the 'Sanskrit Nishtha' Hindi, the Hindi which is derived from Sanskrit and draws its nourishment from the latter, is our *Rashtra Bhasha*, our current national language. In adopting Hindi as the National tongue of Hindudom no humilation or any invidious distinction is implied as regards other provincial tongues. We are all as attached to our provincial tongues as to Hindi and they will all grow and flourish in their respective spheres. It must also be remembered that Hindi is not made a national language to order. The fact is that long before either the English or even the Moslems stepped into India, Hindi in its general form had already come to occupy the position of a national tongue throughout Hindustan.
9. The *Nagari* shall be the national script of Hindudom.
10. The Hindu Mahasabha is a National Organistion of Hindudom. The Hindu Mahasabha is not a Hindu Mission. It leaves religious questions regarding theism, monotheism, pantheism or even atheism to be discussed

and determined by the different Hindu schools of religious persuasions. The sphere of its activity is far more comprehensive than that of an exclusively religious body. The Hindu Mahasabha identifies itself with the national life of Hindudom in all its entirety, in all its social, economical, cultural and above all political aspects and is pledged to protect and promote all that contributes to the freedom, strength and glory of the Hindu nation; and as an indispensable means to that end to attain '*Purna Swaraja*', absolute political independence of Hindustan by all legitimate and proper means.

11. The Hindu Mahasabha must continue its mission even after Hindustan is politically free. It grew up of a fundamental necessity of national life and not of any ephemeral incident. The constructive side of its aim and objects make it amply clear that its mission is as abiding as the fife of the nation itself.[28]

The mere formation of the ideals and ideology of the Hindu movement is not adequate. What is required is an entire orientation of the public activities of the Hindu people so as to revolutionise the conception of the Indian State. The concept is beyond doubt that "the Hindus are a nation by themselves." If the United States with the warring crowds of Negroes, Germans and Anglo Saxons, with a common past not exceeding four or five centuries put together can be called a nation, then the Hindus must be entitled to be recognised as a nation par excellence. So far as other minorities in India are concerned, there cannot be much difficulty in arriving at an Indian National consolidation. The Parsees have ever been working shoulder to shoulder with the Hindus against the English domination. The Christians too have not attached a millstone round our neck. Same is true of the Jews. As regards the Muslims in India, Savarkar was of the view that real unity can only come when Mohammedans need it! Henceforth, the Hindu formula for Hindu Moslem unity is only this: "if you come, with you; if you don't, without you; and if you oppose, inspite of you the Hindus will continue to fight for their National Freedom as best as they can![29]

This fact was not confined merely to the freedom movement. Savarkar believed that nationalism is but an inevitable step towards the goal of humanity and Pan-human State. The world is our country and humanity is our religion and patriotism. Therefore, Savarkar warned the Hindus, "Before you make out a case for unity, you must make out a case for survival as a national or a social human unit." But he asked the Hindus to be on their guard against the Mumbo Jumbo of universalism and non-violence which crush the faculty even for resisting sin, crime and aggression, nay, kill the very sense of wrong and the power of resistance. The peace and prosperity of the Hindus was the central aim of Savarkarian philosophy, no doubt, but his ideals and ideology never struck at the suppression of minorities! The problems of the minorities is that of only one minority, that is, the Muslims, for whom we had to pay the heavy price of partition of the country. Savarkar further explained his attitude towards the minorities in general. The Parsis, he stated, amongst the other minorities were by race, religion, language and culture, most akin to the Hindus. They had been loyal to India and had made her their only home. They had produced some of the best Indian patriots and revolutionaries like Dadabhai Naoroji and Madame Cama. He, therefore, said that the Parsis would be incorporated into the common Indian state with perfect equal rights and trust. The Christian minority, Savarkar observed, was civil, had no extra territorial political designs against India, was not linguistically and culturally averse to the Hindus and therefore could be politically assimilated with the Hindus. Only the conversation should be made voluntary and on a legitimate basis. As to the Jews in India, he felt, they were too few and had given no political or cultural troubles and were not to proselytise people. They would be friendly towards the Hindus who had sheltered them when homeless, and could easily be assimilated in a common Indian State.

Savarkar's pro-Hindu standard and his propagation of the idea of Hindu Rashtra has often been interpreted as his support to the Two Nation Theory, and thus attempts have been made to him with M.A. Jinnah. But it is not a fact! All that Savarkar wished for was the consolidation of the Hindus on a single platform. It became all the more important with Muslim League's Resolution on Pakistan.

It was both resented and ridiculed by the Hindus. However, the political aggression of the Muslims dates back to the closing decade of the nineteenth century. On one point we may agree that with the rise of the nationalist movement, the British statesmen grew apprehensive about the safety and stability of their Empire in India. To check the growth of a united national feeling in the country, they decided to follow more actively the policy of 'Divide and Rule', and to divide the people along religious line, in other words, to encourage communal and separatist tendencies in Indian politics. The British rulers did play an important role in the promotion, spread, growth, and the ultimate partial success of communalism in modern India. Their role became crucial precisely because they held state power, a crucial determinant in the political fortunes of any political ideology or movement. But it is also true and obvious that the British policy of 'Divide and Rule' could succeed because something in the internal social, economic, cultural and political conditions of society favoured its success.

It may sound strange to many that Savarkar and Jinnah instead of being opposed to each other on the one nation *versus* two-nation's theory were in complete agreement about it. Savarkar may have also referred to the Hindus and the Muslims as the two antagonistic nations living in India side by side. He may have even alleged that as long as the Mohammedans lived in India in the capacity of the alien rulers, so long, to be willing to live with them like brothers was to acknowledge national weakness.[30] Yet, despite all odds, the fact remains that Jinnah wanted to cut India into two, Pakistan and Hindustan, the Muslim nation to occupy Pakistan and the Hindu nation to occupy Hindustan. Savarkar, on the other hand, insisted that although there are two nations in India, she shall not be divided into two parts, one for Muslims and the other for the Hindus; that the two nations shall dwell in one country and live under the mantic of one single constitution with special provisions, enabling the Hindu nation to predominate whereas the Muslim nation would have a subordinate position.

In the struggle for political power between the two nations, the rule of the game which Savarkar prescribes 'one man one vote', be the man Hindu or Muslim. In his scheme, a Muslim is to have no advantage or privilege which a Hindu does not enjoy. Minority status is no justification for privilege, and majority cannot be subjected to penalty. The State will guarantee the Muslims defined measure of political power in the form of Muslim religion and Muslim culture. But the State will not guarantee secured seats in the Legislature or in the Administration and, if such guarantee is insisted upon by the Muslims, such guaranteed quota is not to exceed their proportion to the general population.

This alternative of Savarkar for the formation of Pakistan has about it a frankness, boldness and definiteness which distinguishes it from the irritating vagueness and indefiniteness which characterizes the Congress declarations about minority rights. Savarkar's scheme has at least the merit of telling the Muslims, thus far, and no further. On the other hand, the Congress has been treating the Muslims and the minority question as a game in diplomacy, if not in duplicity.[31]

In all his endeavours to promote the concept of Hindu nation, his social objective remained a Hindu mind freed from blind religiosity, spiritualism and unquestioning belief in the scriptures. Savarkar was an advocate of temporal Hindutva that could be tested on the touchstone of intellect. He separated Hindutva from religion and equated it with nationalism and science. An important part of Savarkar's propagation of Hindutva was his premise that change of religion meant change of nationhood. Conversion of Religion is sub-version of Nationhood. Here Savarkar played a triple role the thinker of Hindutva, the protector of Hindutva and the organizer of Hindus. Savarkar asserted that conversion from Hinduism does not merely consist of dismissal of idol-worship, polytheism, the revelation of the Vedas and the divinity of Rama and Krishna. It also brings in its wake the abandonment of emotional attitudes which are the very bulwark of this nation. It is for this reason that Savarkar proclaimed that conversions from Hinduism are a direct attack on India's nationhood and warned that such conversions would lead to a dismemberment of this nation. History also bears him out. Karan Singh, former Maharaja of Kashmir, has narrated how the Muslims living in the Kashmir Valley approached the then Maharaja of Kashmir with a petition that they were former Hindus, forcibly converted by foreign invaders and would like to return to their parent religion. The Maharaja welcomed the idea but his family-priest threatened to commit suicide at his door if he took back the Muslims into the Hindu fold. The matter was dropped.[32]

The India of Savarkar's dreams was one in which all citizens would have equal rights and obligations irrespective of caste, creed, race or religion provided they avow and owe an exclusive and devoted allegiance to the State. All minorities would be given effective safeguards to protect their language, religions, culture, etc. but none of them would be allowed to create a State within a State or to encroach upon the legitimate rights of the majority. Also, the fundamental rights of freedom of speech, freedom of conscience, of worship of association etc. would be enjoyed by all citizens alike; whatever restrictions would be imposed on them in the interest of the public peace and order or national emergency would not be based on any religious or racial considerations alone but common national grounds. One man one vote would be the general rule irrespective of caste, creed, race or religion. There would be joint electorates. Services would go by merit alone. Primary education will be free and compulsory. Every minority would have separate schools to train their children in their own tongue; their religious and cultural institutions would receive government help also for these, but always in proportion to the taxes they pay into the common exchequer. The residuary powers would be vested in the Central Government. *Nagari* would be the national script, Hindi, the *lingua franca* and Sanskrit, the *Devabhasha* of India.

Thus Savarkar's India would be a democratic state in which the countrymen belonging to different religions, sects or races would be treated with perfect equality and none would be allowed to dominate others or would be deprived of his just and equal rights of free citizenship, so long as every one discharges the common obligation which one owes to the state as a whole. Hindustan, the Motherland and Holyland of the Hindus, from the Indus to the seas, would be an organic undivided state. The appellation of this Bharat Bhoomi would remain as Bharat of Hindustan. In Savarkar's India none would dare convert Hindus by fraud or force. Everywhere the Indians would be respected as citizens of a great nation. In that

India relative non-violence would be regarded as a Virtue. The Hindus would be a casteless society, a consolidated, modernized and up-to-date nation. Their marriage customs would be secularized and voluntary inter-caste marriages would be freely performed.

Savarkar's Hindutva is not a narrow creed. It is claimed to be rationalistic and scientific. It is not opposed to humanism and universalism. He quotes Tukaram's statement, "The limits of the universe—there the frontiers of my country lie." In a letter to Guy A. Alfred, editor of *The World*, Savarkar wrote, "I hold that although Mankind must march on through nationalism and federalism, through larger and larger statal incorporations to their ultimate political goal, yet the goal is not and cannot be nationalism but Humanism, neither more nor less. The ideal of all political science and art must be a Human government based on equality of rights and duties, which ought to be our ultimate political goal."[33]

REFERENCES

1. Swami Vivekananda, Lectures from Colombo, *The Complete Works of Swami Vivekananda*, Vol. III (Calcutta: Advaita Ashrama), 1994, pp. 103-104.
2. *Ibid.*, Vol. VI, p. 416.
3. B.R. Ambedkar, *Thoughts on Pakistan* (Lahore: Mustafa), 1945, p. 123.
4. Dhanajaya Keer, *Veer Savarkar, op. cit.*, p. 262.
5. V.D. Savarkar, *Hindutva, op. cit.*, p. 3.
6. *Ibid.*, pp. 72-73.
7. *Ibid.*
8. C.B. Fawcett, *Frontiers—A Study in Political Geography* (London: OUP), 1921, p. 5.
9. Harold Laski, *Grammar of Politics* (London: Allen), 1948, pp. 219-20.
10. Quoted in Isarel Zangwill, *Principles of Nationalities* (London: Heinemann), 1920, p. 28.
11. *Ibid.*
12. G.P. Gooch, *Nationalism* (London: Longman), 1945, p. 7.
13. V.D. Savarkar, *Hindutva, op. cit.*, pp. 10-85.
14. *Ibid.*
15. *Ibid.*
16. *Ibid.*
17. *Ibid.*
18. S.R. Namdar, *Parasnis Gopal Krishan Gokhale* (Bombay: Popular), 1956.
19. *Sarojini Speeches and Writings* (Madras: G.A. Natesan and Co.), 1940, p. 26.

20. O.P. Ralhan (ed.), *Hindu Mahasabha*, Vol. I (New Delhi: Anmol), 1997, p. 80.
21. George, S. Arundale, *The Maratha*, 22 July, 1942.
22. B.R. Ambedkar, *Thoughts on Pakistan, op. cit.*, p. 333.
23. V.D. Savarkar, *Hindutva, op. cit.*
24. *Ibid.*
25. V.D. Savarkar, *Hindu Rashtra Darshan* (Bombay: Veer Savarkar Prakashan), 1974, p. 77.
26. *Ibid.*, p. 4.
27. *Ibid.*, pp. 78-80.
28. *Ibid.*, pp. 81-88.
29. *Ibid.*, p. 23.
30. V.D. Savarkar, *The Indian War of Independence, op. cit.*, p. 75.
31. B.R. Ambedkar, *Thoughts on Pakistan, op. cit.*, pp. 131-132.
32. Jyoti Tehran, *Veer Savarkar, op. cit.*, p. 116.
33. V.D. Savarkar, *Hindutva, op. cit.*

4

HINDU MAHASABHA

Whereas the Muslim League was formed in 1906, it was not before 1915 that the first session of the All India Hindu Mabasabha was held at Hardwar. The ground for it was prepared by the organisation of provincial Hindu Sabhas in the Punjab and Bengal. The first Hindu Sabha was established in the Punjab in 1907. The same year a session of the United Bengal Conference was held. The circumstances which led the Hindus of East Bengal and the Punjab to form provincial organisations for the protection of their rights and interests deserve to be stated at some length.

The Partition of Bengal in 1905 and the formation of the Muslim League at Dacca in December, 1906, were followed by communal riots in which much Hindu property was looted and Hindu women abducted by Muslim hooligans and forcibly converted to Islam. For the protection of their property and the honour of their womenfolk the Hindus organised Anushilan Samities in many towns of East Bengal. In 1907 at the session of the United Bengal Conference two resolutions were passed which were indicative of the new consciousness and awakening that was coming over the Hindus. Col. U N. Mukerji told the Bengal Hindus that they were on the verge of becoming 'a dying race'.[1] During the preceding fifty years the Hindus had dwindled from 55 to 45 per cent of the total population of Bengal. If this serious decline in population was not checked, the future of the Hindus was dark indeed. One of the resolutions adopted at the Conference expressed apprehension at the steady decrease in the population of the Hindus, and the second urged the people to take practical steps for the amelioration of the depressed classes.

In the Punjab, the Hindus were goaded to organise themselves by the injustices that were done to them by the Government in the matter of the distribution of government patronage and the highly disadvantageous position in which they found themselves as the result of measures like the Land Alienation Act being placed on the statute book. In a word, it can be said that the highly preferential treatment accorded to the Muslims by the Government in the matter of civil appointments and the increasingly voracious appetite of the Muslims for more favours encouraged by the British policy of favouring them led the communally minded among the Hindus to think of strengthening and integrating the Hindu community by establishing the Hindu Sabha.

The aims and objects of the first Hindu Sabha were founded in the Punjab which were modest. Stated briefly, they were: (i) promotion of brotherly feelings among the various sections of the Hindu community; (ii) improvement of the moral, intellectual and material conditions of the Hindus; and (iii) looking after and promotion of the general interests of the Hindu community.

The next important step towards the birth of the All India Hindu Mahasabha was the holding of the first Punjab Provincial Conference at Lahore in 1909. It was attended by about 800 delegates from different parts of the province. Lala Lajpat Rai took a prominent part in its deliberations, and made a long speech on the desirability of promoting the sentiment of Hindu unity and Hindu nationality among the Hindus.

From that speech it was clear that the aim of the contemplated All-India Hindu Sabha was nothing more than to organise the Hindu community for the purpose of taking united action for the protection of their rights as a community and formulate public opinion on questions affecting the community as a whole. Lalaji held, and rightly so, that in the then existing political conditions in the country the Hindus were perfectly justified in taking care of the interests of their own community.

The central aim of the Mahasabha has all along been to organise, consolidate and strengthen the Hindu community all over the country for the security and protection of their legitimate nights as a community. There does not seem to be anything wrong in it;

every community has a right to organise itself for the promotion of its interests as a community. The trouble arises when the alleged interests of one community are found to clash with those of other communities and each takes up an attitude of exclusiveness towards the other. In this clash of interests, fancied or real, national interests are bound to suffer, and the evils of communalism begin to manifest themselves. For example, in a speech Lala Lajpat Rai referred to the Hindus as constituting a Nation on the ground that they were united by a common civilization and culture.

The next milestone in the evolution of the Hindu Mahasabha was the second session of the Punjab Hindu Conference held at Delhi in 1912. In the course of his Presidential address Lala Shadi Lal said: "Suffice it so say that the events of the past four or five years prove beyond the shadow of doubt that with a body which could speak with the authority of the entire Hindu community behind its back and resist the aggressive action of the Muslim League, the Hindus would not have been in the plight in which they find themselves at present."[2] But still no concrete step was taken to organise the Hindus on an all India basis. It was at the third session of the Punjab Hindu Conference held at Ambala in 1913 that a resolution was passed to the effect that a general conference of the Hindus be held at Hardwar on the occasion of the Kumbh Mela in 1915. Thus a Reception Committee was organised at Dehra Dun and the first session of the Hindu Sabha was held at Hardwar in 1915. It was designated as the Akhil Bharatiya Hindu Sabha. Its President, Maharaja Mohendra Nandi of Kasimbazar observed as follows in the course of his address: "If, therefore, we make efforts to set our house in order to hold closer together the scattered units of our faith, it cannot imply a menace to any other community or faith."[3]

According to Indra Prakash the historian of the Hindu Mahasabha and the Hindu Movement, the uplift of the depressed classes and the reform of the caste system figured prominently in the programme of work chalked out in the first session at Hardwar.[4] This shows as conceived earlier, the Mahasabha was more interested in social, cultural and religious problems facing the Hindus than the political ones. So far as the latter were concerned, they were content to leave them to the Congress. Many of its leaders like Lala Lajpat Rai and Pundit Madan Mohan Malaviya were staunch Congress leaders, and their sessions were generally held alongside Congress sessions. It was not before 1928 that the Mahasabha began to adopt a somewhat independent attitude on political issues. What led to this departure from the hitherto existing practice was the refusal of the Mahasabha to agree to the League demand for the separation of Sind from Bombay into a separate province where the Muslims would be in an absolute majority. Before discussing this issue, mention may be made of the impetus given to the movement by the communal riots which broke out in a virulent form in the country after the withdrawal of the Non-cooperation Movement and the collapse of the Khilafat Movement as a result of the abolition of the Khilafat by Kamal Pasha when be came to power in Turkey.

The Hindu Mahasabha did not make any appreciable progress during the first half decade of its existence; it failed to catch the imagination of the Hindu masses. When Gandhiji launched the first Non-cooperation Movement in 1920, the Mahasabha languished still more; the attention of the people was engrossed by the stirring events which took place in connection with the Non-cooperation Movement. The communal riots which broke out in various parts of the country after the abrupt withdrawal of his movement by Gandhiji, and the set back the Khilafat Movement received as a result of the abolition of Khilafat by Mustafa Kamal Pasha in Turkey, however proved to be God sent so far as the fortunes of the Mahasabha were concerned. When the Khilafat Movement was at its height, fanatic Moplahs of Malabar thought that the Khilafat Raj had come. They began to convert Malabar Hindus forcibly, making them under go circumcision, looting Hindu property and abducting Hindu women. The atrocities committed by the Moplahs on their Hindu compatriots shocked the Hindus all over the country, and one of the leaders, Dr. Moonje joined the Mahasabha. The terrible events in Malabar were followed by the tragedy of Multan and the roits at Kohat, Bannu and other places. These events gave a great impetus to the Mahasabha movement; there was great accession of strength to its ranks. Leaders like Lala Lajpat Rai, Pundit Madan Mohan Malaviya, Bhai Parmanand, M.R. Jayakar and N.C. Kelkar began to take a more lively interest in its affairs and joined it. The world of the Hindus resounded with the cry of Sangathan or organisation and consolidation. A new period began in the history of the movement.

To Sangathan was added *Shuddhi* or the movement to bring back to the Hindu fold former converts to Islam and Christianity and their descendants. The Arya Samaj had already been engaged in the work of *Shuddhi*. Now the Mahasabha also made it a part of its activities. At its session held at Benaras in 1923 under the Presidentship of Pundit Madan Mohan Malaviya, which was attended by 1500 delegates drawn from different parts of the country and included representatives of the Sikhs, the Jains, the Buddhists, the Sanatanists, the Arya Samajists, and even the Parsis, resolutions were passed stressing the need for removing untouchability and admitting to their old faith Hindu converts to other religions.[5] The news that about four and a half lakhs of Muslim Rajputs known as Malkhanas were ready to join Hindu society greatly enraged and infuriated the Muslim Maulvis who sent their own preachers to keep them within the Islamic fold. In reply to the Hindu Movement of *Sangathan* and *Shuddhi* the Muslims started their own movement of *Tanzeem* and *Tabligh* i.e. organisation and propagation. The communal atmosphere became highly surcharged. A Muslim fanatic who pretended to be a would be convert to Hinduism stabbed to death Swami Shraddhanand, a highly respected Arya Samaj leader. His murder was followed by the assassination of several other leaders and workers of the Arya Samaj. This led the National Congress to adopt a resolution at its Gauhati session calling upon the working Committee to take immediate steps, in consultation with Hindu and Muslim leaders, to devise measures for the removal of the deplorable differences between the two communities. Nothing came out of this resolution.

At this time the leadership of the Hindu Mahasabha passed into the hands of Moonje and Bhai Parmanand. A new era of struggle, opposition, isolation, self-determination and consolidation may be said to have begun with the new leadership. It was an era of struggle and opposition in so far as the Mahasabha had to meet with the stiff opposition of the Muslims and Christians on the one side, and that of the Congress on the other. It was a period of isolation and self-determination in so far as it gave up the practice of leaving political questions to the Congress and began to take an independent attitude towards them. This attitude was forced on it by the pro-Muslim policy of the Congress and its inability to safeguard the interests of the Hindus. One or two instances may be cited to illustrate the point. It was against the wishes of the Congress and leaders like Pundit Madan Mohan Malaviya that the Mahasabha should oppose the Muslim League demand for the Separation of Sind from Baluchistan and the extension of reform to N. W. F. P. A section of Mahasabha favoured cooperation with the Simon Commission finding that the policies of the Swaraj party were inimical to Hindu interests. Some Hindu Sabha leaders felt that Hindu interests were not safe in Congress hands, and that the Mahasabha should set-up its own candidates for the various legislatures in the country. As a compromise, the decision was taken that the Mahasabha should not lend its support to those Congress nominees who were not likely to support the Hindu cause. The result of the opposition on the part of the Hindu Sabha was that the Swarajists suffered many reverses in the elections held in 1926. Several Hindu leaders were returned to the Central Legislative Assembly as Independents or Responsivists. Lala Lajpat Rai, Pundit Malaviya and Dr. Moonje were the most important among them. It is worth noting that these persons did not form a rival Hindu party, and were content to call themselves Independents. On crucial occasions they worked in full cooperation with the Swarajists.

It may also be added that while the Congress did not agree to participate in the first Round Table Conference in London, the Mahasabha was represented by its President, Dr. B. S. Moonje. It is also worth noting that while the Congress remained neutral on the Communal Award given by Ramsay Macdonald, neither, accepting nor rejecting it, the Hindu Mahasabha repudiated it as being most unfair and unjust to the Hindus. It carried its opposition to the Award to the extent of sending a long cable to the League of Nations, requesting to intervene and see that the League principles were applied to the solution of the communal problem in India. The rift with the Congress became complete with the assumption of the leadership of the Mahasabha by Vinayak Damordar Sarvarkar after his release from internment in 1937.

Bhai Parmanand puts in a nutshell the aim of the Mahasabha and the reasons for it. He writes: "I was firmly convinced that the way to this salvation (that of India) was to make the Hindu community, as a whole, strong and powerful. The stronger the Hindus would grow, the greater would be the chance of the other communities combining with them in working for the common good of the country. If, on the other hand, the Hindus remained weak as they are...no other community will ever desire cooperation with them."[6]

In the course of his Presidential address at the session of the Mahasabha held at Lahore in 1936. His Holiness Shri Shankaracharya struck a pan-Hindu note. The Hindu Mahasabha should be considered as the representative not only of the Hindus by birth or of the Hindus in Hindustan, but also the representative of the Hindus abroad and particularly of those who have, by voluntary choice, enlisted themselves as Hindus and whom we should consider as Hindus by adoption. The Mahasabha took the momentous step to establish close contacts with Hindus settled in foreign lands and thereby tried to put an end to the cultural isolation of the Hindus in India with those outside. As a step in the desired direction it sent its representatives to Japan to attend the 26th centenary of Lord Buddha and pay homage to his memory. Buddhist delegates from Ceylon and Burma came to attend the annual sessions of the Hindu Mahasabha. Contacts were also established with the Hindus of Nepal and her ruling chief.

G.V. Ketkar, Hony. Secretary of the Hindu Mahasabha, describes the aims and objects of the Mahasabha in the following words:

'To organise and consolidate all sections of the Hindu society into one organic whole; to protect and promote Hindu interests whenever and wherever necessary; to remove untouchability and generally to ameliorate and improve the condition of the so-called depressed classes among the Hindus; to revive and promote the glorious ideals of Hindu womenhood; to promote cow protection; to improve the physique of the Hindus and promote martial spirit among them by establishing military schools and organising volunteer corps; to reclaim all those who have left the Hindu fold; to found orphanages and rescue homes for orphans and homeless women; generally to take steps for promoting religious, educational, social, economic and political interests and rights of the Hindus. To promote good feelings between the Hindus and non-Hindu communities in Hindustan, and to act in a friendly way with them with a view to evolving a united and self-governing Bharateeya Nation based on equality of civic rights and duties irrespective of caste and creed.[7]

Though the communal riots which broke out in the country after the withdrawal of the Non-cooperation Movement gave much impetus to the Hindu Mahasabha, the latter did not make great headway; it remained a more or less impotent body without any mass support. Even the leadership of Bhai Parmanand and Dr. Moonje failed to make it a virile body. It was not before the advent Vinayak Damodar Savarkar who was released after nearly 14 years of exile in the Andamans Jail and 13 years of internment in his home district of Ratnagiri, that it had a really virile and clear cut programme for the regeneration of the Hindu community. He came at a time when 'the turn of events in the political arena was giving rise to the as yet unexpressed feeling among the Hindus that the Congress to which they had given their unqualified support was going after the will-of-the-wisp in placating the ever growing demands of the Muslim League and was thereby sacrificing the rights and interests of the majority community. Savarkar used all his great talents of speech and organisation to impress upon his co-religionists the dangerous consequences of this policy and the effect it would have upon their future. He placed before them the idea and programme of Hindu Nationalism in forceful and convincing language as had never been done before. The concept of Hindutva on which his programme is based may be regarded as his chief contribution to political thought.

The Definition of the Word 'Hindu'

As the whole superstructure of the mission and the function of the Hindu Mahasabha rests on the correct definition of the word 'Hindu', we must first of all make it clear what 'Hindutva' really means. Once the scope and the meaning of the word is defined and understood, a number of misgivings in our own camp are easily removed, as well as the misunderstandings and objections raised against us from the camp of our opponents. Fortunately for us, after a lot of wandering in wilderness, a definition of the word 'Hindu' is not only historically and logically as sound as is possible in the cases of such comprehensive terms, but is also eminently workable, is already hit upon when 'Hindutva' was defined as:

"Everyone who regards and claims this Bharatbhoomi from the Indus to the Seas as his Fatherland and Holyland is a Hindu". Here I must point out that it is rather loose to say that any person professing any religion of Indian origin is a Hindu. Because that is only one aspect of Hindutva. The second and equally essential constituent of the concept of Hindutva cannot be ignored if we want to save the definition from getting overlapping and unreal. It is not enough that a person should profess any religion of Indian origin, i.e. recognize Hindustan as his Holyland, but he must also recognize it as his too, his Fatherland as well."[8]

It is these two constituents taken together that constitute Hindutva and distinguish it from any other people in the world. That is why the Japanese and the Chinese, for example, do not and cannot regard themselves as fully identified with the Hindus. Both of them regard our Hindustan as their Holyland, the land which was the cradle of their religion, but they do not and cannot look upon Hindustan as their Fatherland too. They are our co-religionists; but are not and cannot be our countrymen too. We Hindus are not only co-religionists, but even countrymen of each other. The Japanese and the Chinese have a different ancestry, language, culture, history and country of their own, which are not so integrally bound up with us as to constitute a common national life. In a religious assembly of the Hindus, in any Hindu-Dharma-Mahasabha they can join with us as our brothers in faith, having a common Holyland. But they will not and cannot take a common part or have a common interest in a Hindu Mahasabha which unites Hindus together and represents their national life.

A definition must in the main respond to reality. Just as by the first constituent of Hindutva, the possession of a common Holyland—the Indian Mahommedans, Jews, Christians, Parsees, etc. are excluded from claiming themselves as Hindu which in reality also they do not—in spite of their recognizing Hindustan as their Fatherland, so also on the other hand the second constituent of the definition that of possessing a common Fatherland excludes the Japanese, the Chinese and others from the Hindu fold in spite of the fact of their having a Holyland in common with us.

From this correct definition of Hindutva it necessarily follows that we should take all possible care to restrict the use of the word 'Hindu' to its defined and definite general meaning only and avoid misusing it in any sectarian sense. In common parlance even our esteemed leaders and writers who on the one hand are very particular in emphasizing that our non-Vedic religious schools are also included in the common Hindu brotherhood, commit on the other hand, the serious mistake of using such expressions as 'Hindus and Sikhs', 'Hindus and Jains', denoting thereby unconsciously that the Vedics or the Sanatanists only are Hindus and this quite unawares inculcate the deadly virus of separation in the minds of the different constituents of our religious 'brotherhood, defeating our own eager desire to consolidate them all into a harmonious and organic whole'. Confusion in words leads to confusion in thoughts.

If we take good care not to identify the term 'Hindu' with the major Vedic section of our people alone, our non-Vedic brethren such as the Sikhs, the Jains and others will find no just reason to resent the application of the word 'Hindu' in their case also. Those who hold to the opinion that Sikhism, Jainism and such other religions that go to form our Hindu brotherhood are neither the branches of nor originated from the Vedas but are independent religions by themselves need not cherish any fear or suspicion of losing their independence as a religious school by being called Hindus if that application is rightly used only to denote all those who own India, this Bharatbhoomi, as their Holyland and Fatherland. Whenever we want to discriminate the constituents of Hindudom as a whole we should designate them as 'Vedics and Sikhs', 'Vedics and Jains', etc. But to say 'Hindus and Sikhs', 'Hindus and Jains' is as self-contradictory and misleading as to say 'Hindus and Brahmins' or 'Jains and Digambers' or 'Sikhs and Akalees,'. Such a harmful misuse of the word Hindu should be carefully avoided especially in the speeches, resolutions and records of our Hindu Mahasabha.

The Hindus are Nation by Themselves

"How the Hindus who differ so much amongst themselves in every detail of life could at all be called a nation as such?" To them my reply writes Savarkar is that no people on the earth are so homogenous as to present perfect uniformity in language, culture, race and religion. A people is marked out as a nation by themselves not so much by the absence of any heterogeneous differences amongst themselves as by the fact of their differing from other peoples more markedly than they differ amongst themselves. Even those who deny the fact that the Hindus could be called a nation by themselves, do recognize Great Britain, the United States, Russia, Germany and other peoples as nations. What is the test by which those peoples are called nations by themselves? Take Great Britain as an example. There are at any rate three different languages; they have fought amongst themselves dreadfully in the past, there are to be found the traces of different seeds and bloods and races.[9]

If you say that in spite of it all they are a nation because they possess a common country, a common language, a common culture and common Holyland, then the Hindus too possess a common country so well marked out as Hindustan, a common language, the Sanskrit from which all their current languages are derived or are nourished, and which forms even today the common language of their scriptures and literature and which is held in esteem as the sacred reservoir of ancient scriptures and the tongue of their forefathers. By 'Anuloma' and 'Pratiloma' marriages their seed and blood continues to get comingled ever since the days of Manu. Their social festivals and cultural forms are not less common than those we find in England. They possess a common Holyland.

The *Vedic Rishis* are their common pride, their Grammarians Panini and Patanjali, their Poets Bhavabhooti and Kalidas, their heroes Shree Ram and Shree Krishna, Shivaji and Pratap, Guru

Govind and Banda are a source of common inspiration. Their Prophets, Buddha and Mahaveer, Kanad and Shankar, are held in common esteem. Like their ancient and sacred language—the Sanskrit—their scripts also are fashioned on the same basis and the *Nagari* script has been the common vehicle of their sacred writings since centuries in the past. Their ancient and modern history is common. They have friends and enemies in common. They have faced common dangers and won victories in common. Whether in national glory or national disasters, national despairs or national hope, the Hindus are welded together through common life and a common habitat. Above all, the Hindus are bound together by the dearest, most sacred and most enduring bonds of a common Fatherland and a common Holyland, and these two being identified with one and the same country, our Bharatbhumi, our India, the National oneness and homogeneity of the Hindus have been doubly sure.

If the United States with the warring crowds of Negroes, Germans and Anglo-saxons, with a common past not exceeding four or five centuries put together, can be called a nation, then the Hindus must be entitled to be recognized as a nation par excellence. Verily the Hindus as a people differ most markedly from any other people in the world than they differ amongst themselves. All tests whatsoever of a common country, race, religion, and language that go to entitle a people to form a nation, entitle the Hindus with greater emphasis to that claim. And whatever differences divide the Hindus amongst themselves are rapidly disappearing owing to their awakening of the national consciousness and the Sanghatan and the social reform movements to today.[10]

Mahasabha is not a Hindu Dharma Sabha but Hindu Rashtra Sabha

The Mahasabha though only indirectly concerned with Hinduism, as one of the many aspects of Hindutva, is mainly concerned with other aspects of Hindutva resulting from the second constituent of possessing a common Fatherland. The Mahasabha is not therefore primarily a Hindu-Dharam Sabha but is pre-eminently a Hindu Rashtra Sabha and is a Pan-Hindu organisation shaping the destinies of the Hindu nation in all its social, political and cultural aspects. It leaves religious questions regarding theism, monotheism and pantheism or even atheism to be discussed and determined by the different Hindu schools of religious persuasions. As a national Hindu body, it will of course propagate and defend the National Hindu church comprising each and all religions of Hindustani origin against any non-Hindu attack or encroachment. Its sphere of activity is far more comprehensive than that of an exclusively religious body.

The Hindu Mahasabha identifies itself with the national life of Hindudom in all its entirety social, economical, cultural and political aspects—and is pledged to protect and promote all that contributes to the freedom, strength and glory of the Hindu nation, and as an indispensable means to that end to attain *Purna Swarajya* absolute political Independence of Hindustan by all legitimate and proper means.[11]

Mahasabha not a Communal or Anti-Indian Organisation

Some scholars, who look down upon the Mahasabha as a communal, narrow and anti-Indian body because it represents Hindudom and tries to protect its just rights, forget the fact that communal and parochial are only relative terms and do not by themselves imply a condemnation or curse. Are not they themselves who swear by the name of Indian Nationalism in season and out season liable to the same charge of parochialness? If the Mahasabha represents the Hindu Nation only, they claim to represent the Indian Nation alone.

But is not the concept of an Indian Nation itself a parochial conception in relation to Human State? In fact the Earth is our Motherland and Humanity our Nation. Nay, the Vedantist goes further and claims this Universe for his country and all manifestations from the stars to the stone his own self, says Tukaram ! Why then take the Himalayas to cut us off from the rest of mankind, deem ourselves as a separate nation as Indians and fight with every other country and the English in particular who after all are our brothers in Humanity! Why not sacrifice Indian interests to those of the British Empire which is a larger political synthesis? The fact is that all patriotism is more or less parochial and communal and is responsible for dreadful wars throughout human history. Thus the Indian patriots who instead of starting and joining some movement of an universal state, stop short of it, join an Indian Movement and yet continue to mock at the Hindu Sanghatan, as narrow and communal and parochial, succeed only in mocking at themselves.

But if it is said in justification of Indian patriotism that the people living in India are more akin to each other bound by the ties of a common ancestry, language, culture, history etc. than they are to any other people outside India and therefore we Indians feel it our first duty to protect our nation from the political domination and aggression of other non-Indian nations, then, the same reason could be applied justify the Hindu Sanghatan Movement as well.

No movement is condemnable simply because it is sectional so long as it tries to defend the just and fundamental rights of a particular nation or people or community against the unjust and overbearing aggression of other human aggregates and does not infringe on equal and just rights and liberties of others, it cannot be condemned or looked down simply because the nation or community is a smaller aggregate in itself.

But when a nation or community treads upon the rights of sister nations or communities and aggressively stands in the way of forming larger associations and aggregates of mankind, its nationalism or communalism becomes condemnable from a human point of view. This is the acid test of distinguishing a justifiable nationalism or communalism from an unjust and harmful one. The Hindu Sanghatan Movement, call it national, communal or parochial as you like, stands as much justified by this real test as our Indian Patriotism can be.[12]

Hindu Mahasabha is Perfectly National in Its Outlook

For, what does the Hindu Mahasabha aim at? As the national representative body of Hindudom it aims at an all-round regeneration of the Hindu people. But the absolute political independence of Hindustan is a *sine qua non* for an all round regeneration of Hindudom. The fortunes of the Hindus are more inextricably and more closely bound up with India than that of any other Non-Hindu sections of our country-men. After all the Hindus are the bedrock on which an Indian independent state could be built.

According to Savarkar "To a Hindu, India is all in all of his National Being. That is the reason why the Hindus predominate in the struggle for the overthrow of the political domination of England over this country. It is the Hindus who went to the gallows, faced transportation to the Andamans by hundreds and got imprisoned by thousands in the fight for the liberation of Hindustan. Even the Indian National Congress owes its growth to Hindu brain and to Hindu sacrifice.

A Hindu patriot worth the name cannot but be an Indian patriot as well. In this sense the consolidation and the independence of Hindu Nation is but another name for the independence of the Indian Nation as a whole. For the Hindu Sanghatanists know fully well that no regeneration of Hindudom could be brought about and no honour and equal place could be secured for the Hindu Nation amongst the Nations of the world unless Swarajya and Swatantrya are won for Hindusthan, their Fatherland and Holyland."[13]

Mahasabhas not the Outcome of a Reaction to Muslim League but of Fundamental Necessity of National Life

Many a superficial critic seem to fancy that the Mahasabha was only contrived to serve as a make weight, as a reaction, check mating the Muslim League or the anti-Hindu policy of the present leaders of the Congress and will be out of court or cease automatically to function as soon as it is shorn of this spurious excuse to exist. But it is clear that it was not the outcome of any frothy effusion, any fussy agitation to remove a grievance here or oppose a seasonal Party there. The fact is that every organism whether individual or social which is living and deserves to survive throws out offensive and defensive organs as soon as it is brought to face adversely changing environments.

The Hindu Nation too as soon as it recovered and freed itself from the suffocating grip of the Pseudo Nationalistic ideology of the Congress brand developed a new organ to battle in the struggle for existence under the changed conditions of modern age. This was the Hindu Mahasabha. It grew up of a fundamental necessity of national life and not of any ephemeral incident. The constructive side of its aims and objects make it amply clear that its mission is as abiding as the life of the Nation itself. But leaving that apart, even the day-to-day necessity of adapting its policy to the ever changing political currents make it incumbent on Hindudom to have an exclusively Hindu organisation independent of any moral or intellectual servility or subservience to any non-Hindu or jointly representative institution, to guard Hindu interest and save them from being jeopardised.[14]

Mahasabha will Continue its Mission even after Hindustan is Politically Free

It is not so only under the present political subjection of Hindustan but it will be all the more necessary to have such an exclusively Hindu organisation to serve as a watch-tower at the gates of Hindudom for at least a couple of centuries to come, even after Hindustan is partially or wholly free and a National Parliament controls its political destiny.

Because, unless something altogether cataclysmic in nature upsets the whole political order of things in the world which practical politics cannot envisage today, all that can be reasonably expected in immediate future is that we Hindus may prevail over England and compel her to recognise India as a self-governing unit with the status contemplated in the West Minister Statute. Now a National Parliament in such a self-governing India can only reflect the electorate as it is, the Hindus and the Moslems as we find them, their relations a bit bettered, perhaps a bit worsened. No realist can be blind to the probability that the extra territorial designs and the secret urge goading on the Moslems to transform India into a Moslem state may at any time confront the Hindustani State even under self-government either with a Civil War or treacherous overtures to alien invaders by the Moslems.

Then again there is every likelihood that there will ever continue, at least for the century to come the danger of fanatical riots, the scramble for services, legislative seats, weightages out of proportion to their population on the part of the Moslem minority and consequently a constant danger threatening internal peace. To checkmate this probability, which if we are wise, we must always keep in view even after Hindustan attains the status of a self-governing country, a powerful and exclusive organisation of Hindudom like the Hindu Mahasabha will always prove a sure and devoted source of strength, a reserve force for the Hindus to fall back upon to voice their grievances more effectively than the joint Parliament can do, to scent danger ahead, to warn the Hindus in time against it and to fight out if need be any treacherous design to which the joint state itself may unwittingly fall a victim.

The history of Canada, of Palestine, of the movement of the young Turks will show you that in every state where two or more such conflicting elements as the Hindus and Moslems in India happen to exist as constituents, the wiser of them has to keep its exclusive organisation intact, strong and watchful to defeat any attempt at the betrayal or the capture of the National State by the opposite party; especially so if that party has extra territorial affinities religious or cultural, with alien bordering states. This tussle between such constituents of such a state must continue till slowly if ever they all learn to get themselves merged by developing a spirit of corporate patriotism into a consolidated nation.

If the Hindus take this realistic truth to heart they will try their utmost to consolidate and strengthen the Pan-Hindu organisation which is already gathering force and has struck its roots deep in the Hindu soil. The nearer you are to Swarajya the more indispensable grows the necessity of a strong and consolidated Pan-Hindu organisation, or rather the stronger grows the Pan-Hindu organisation the nearer it takes you to real "Swa"-Rajya.[15]

The National Constitution of Hindustan

The Hindu Sanghatanists aim to base the future constitution of Hindustan on the following broad principles:

1. Hindustan from the Indus to the Seas will and must remain as an organic nation and integral centralised state.
2. The residuary powers shall be vested in the Central Government.

3. All citizens shall have equal rights and obligations irrespective of caste or creed, race or religion provided they avow and own an exclusive and devoted allegiance to the Hindustani State.
4. The fundamental rights of liberty of speech, liberty of conscience, of worship, of association etc. will be enjoyed by all citizens alike whatever restrictions will be imposed on them in the interest of the public peace and order or national emergency will not be based on any religious or racial considerations alone but on common national ground.
5. "One man one vote", will be the general rule irrespective of caste, creed, race or religion.
6. Representation in the Legislature etc. shall be in proportion to the population of the majority and minorities.
7. Services shall go by merit alone.
8. All minorities shall be given effective safeguards to protect their language, religion, culture etc. but none of them shall be allowed to create 'a state within a state', encroach upon the legitimate rights of the majority.
9. Every minority may have separate schools to train up their children in their own tongue, their own religious or cultural institutions could here and can receive government help but always in proportion to the taxes they pay into the common exchequer.
10. In case the constitution is not based on joint electorates and on the unalloyed national principle of one man one vote, but is based on the communal basis then those minorities who wish to have separate electorates or reserve seats will be allowed to have them, but always in proportion to their population and provided that it does not deprive the majority too of an equal right in proportion to its population.

We believe that our Christian, Parsee, the Jews and other minorities except the Moslems, will be perfectly satisfied with the constitution based on these principles as broadly outlined above. The Christians, the Jews and most eminently the Parsees are associated with us in culture and are too patriotic, while the Anglo-Indians are too sensible to fail to see that no constitution, if it has to keep the integrity, sovereignty and strength of the National State safe, can go any further and that it is all that is really required to safeguard any genuine special interests of the minorities as distinguished from those of the majority. Only that minority will insist on having more and yet more to the last pound of flesh which in fact cherishes secret design to disintegrate the State, to create a state within a state or altogether to subvert the National State and hold all others under its subjection. Fortunately no section of our countrymen belonging to the non-Moslem minorities mentioned above harbours this treasonable design. It is only with regards to the Moslem minority that this cannot be asserted with confidence, and therefore we shall deal separately with it.[16]

REFERENCES

1. J.P. Suda, *Main Currents of Social and Political Thought in India, op. cit.*, p. 43.
2. *Ibid.*, p. 483.
3. *Ibid.*
4. Indra Prakash, *A History of Hindu Mahasabha*, quoted in J,. D. Sudha, *op. cit.*, p. 433.
5. O.P. Ralhan (ed.), *Hindu Mahasabha, op. cit.*, p. 61.
6. *Ibid.*, pp. 180-85.
7. *Indian Annual Register*, 1941, Vol. I, p. 276.
8. V.D. Savarkar, *Hindutva, op. cit.*
9. *Ibid.*
10. *Ibid.*
11. *Ibid.*
12. *Ibid.*
13. *Ibid.*
14. *Ibid.*
15. *Ibid.*
16. *Ibid.*

5

NATIONALISM

Savarkar believes that nationalism is but an inevitable step towards the goal of humanity and Pan-Human state. In 1920 he wrote that he believed in a universal state embracing all mankind and where all men and women would be citizens working for the fruits of the earth, the sun and the land which constitute the real Motherland and Fatherland of Man. In fact he said, the world was our country and humanity was our religion and patriotism. In his youth he wrote that history was to be studied to weld humanity into a World Common Wealth. But while the process and struggle, he said, was going on for welding humanity into a World Commonwealth, the weak people had gone under and the fittest had survived.

"Therefore," Savarkar warned the Hindus, "before you make out a case for unity, you must make out a case for survival as a national or a social human unit."[1] This made him devote all his energy to Hindu Nationalism as he believed that Hindu consolidation was a step inevitable in the realization of the ideal of a Human State or a World Commonwealth. Savarkar stressed this point in a letter to Guy A. Aldred, editor of *The Word*, Glasgow. He said: "I hold that although mankind must march on through nationalism and federalism, through larger and larger statal incorporations to their ultimate political goal, yet the goal is not and cannot be nationalism but humanism, neither more nor less. The ideal of all political science and art must be a Human State."[2] This was a message sent by Savarkar to the World Fellowship over their annual session in 1944, which he could not do for reasons of health.

Being a realist Savarkar, however, warned the Hindus in these words: "As long as the law of evolution that lays down the iron command that 'the weak and the cowards are always the victims of the strong and the courageous' is too persistent and dangerously imminent to be categorically denied by the law of righteousness whose mottos shine brilliantly and beautifully—but as the stars in the heavens do—so long the banner of nationality will refuse to be replaced by that of universality".[3] Savarkar declared in unmistakable terms that as long as the whole world was red in tooth and claw and the national and racial distinction so strong as to make men brutal, so long if India had to live at all a life whether spiritual or political according to the light of her soul, she must not lose the strength born of national and racial cohesion.[4]

Therefore, Savarkar again emphasized: "As long as every other 'Ism' has not disowned its special dogmas, whichever tend into dangerous war cries, so long no cultural or national unit can afford to loosen the bonds, especially those of a common name and a common banner that are the mighty sources of organic cohesion and strength."[5] Though a universal religion without any the least ulterior end in view, it could not, Savarkar observed, eradicate the seeds of animal passions or of political ambitions. He, therefore, asked the Hindus to be on their guard against the Mumbo Jumbo of universalism and non-violence which crush the faculty even of resisting sin, crime and aggression, nay, kill the very sense of wrong and the power of resistance.

Savarkar, therefore asked the Hindus to take universalism cautiously. He observed: "What was the use of a universal faith that instead of soothing the ferociousness and brutal egoism of the nations only excited their lust by leaving India defenseless and unsuspecting?"[6] Nevertheless, describing the glory and grandeur of Buddha, he said: "... but as it is though art ours as truly as Ram or Krishna, or Mahavir had been and as thy words were but echos of yarning of national soul, thy visions, the dreams of our race; even so, if ever the law of righteousness rules triumphant on this our human plane, then thou wilt find that the land that cradled the, and the people that nursed thee, will have contributed most to bring about the consummation if indeed the fact of having contributed thee has not proved that much already."[7] What heaps of books and lakhs of preaching on Buddha could not expound, Savarkar did in a paragraph.[8]

So from the point of view of nationalism, humanism and universalism, Savarkar gave his immortal message to the land of Ram, Krishna, Buddha, Mahavir, Vikramaditya, Maharana Pratap, Shivaji, Guru Gobind Singh, Swami Vivekananda and Tilak: "Therefore, ye, O Hindus, consolidate and strengthen Hindu nationality: not to give wanton offence to any of our non-Hindu compatriots, in fact to anyone in the world but in just an urgent self-defence of our race and land; to render it impossible for others to betray her or to subject her to unprovoked attacks by any of those 'Pan-isms' that are struggling forth from continent to continent". "As long as other communities in India or in the World" Savarkar concluded, "are not respectively planning India first or mankind first, but all are busy in organizing offensive and defensive alliances and combinations on entirely narrow racial or religious or national basis, so long, O Hindus, strengthen if you can those subtle bonds that like nerve-threads bind you in one organic social being. Those of you in a suicidal fit try to cut off the most vital of those ties and dare to disown the name Hindu will find to their cost that in doing so they have cut themselves off from the very source of our racial life and strength."[9]

"Thirty crores of people with India for their basis for operation, for their Fatherland and for their Holyland, with such a history behind them, bound together by ties of a common blood and common culture, can dictate their terms to the whole world. A day will come when mankind will have to face the force. Equally certain it is that whenever the Hindus come to hold such a position whence they could dictate their terms to the whole world—those terms cannot be very different from the terms which the *Gita* dictates or the Buddha lays down. A Hindu is more intensely so, when he seizes to be Hindu; and with a Shankar claims the whole earth for a Benares-*Varanasi Medini*—or with a Tukaram exclaims 'my country? Oh brothers, the limits of the universe—there the frontiers of my country lie,'" sang the poetic soul of Savarkar.[10]

The independence of India for Savarkar was "the independence of our people, our race, our nation."[11] Therefore Indian *Swarajya* or Indian *Swatantrya* meant as far as the Hindu Nation is concerned, the political independence of the Hindus, the freedom which would enable them to grow to their full height. But, at the same time, he declared at the 19th Session of the Hindu Mahasabha held in Ahmedabad in 1937, from the Presidential platform, "Let the Indian State be purely Indian. Let it not recognise any invidious distinction, whatsoever as regards the franchise, public services, offices' taxation on the grounds of religion and race. Let no cognizance be taken whatsoever of a man being Hindu or Mohammedan, Christian or Jew. Let all citizens of that Indian State be treated according to their individual worth, irrespective of their religious or racial percentage in the general population. Let that language and script be the national language and script of that Indian state which are understood by the overwhelming majority of the people as happens in every other state in the world, that is, in England or the United States of America, and let no religious bias be allowed to tamper with that language and script with an enforced and perverse hybridism, whatsoever. Let 'one man one vote' be the general rule irrespective of caste or creed, race or religion. If such an Indian State is kept in view, the Hindu Sanghatanists will, in the interest of the Hindu Sanghatan itself, be the first to offer their whole hearted loyalty to it."[12]

Savarkar was of the opinion that Indian foreign policy should hinge on a very practical stand, on the principle of serving, safeguarding and promoting national self-interest. He averred that it should not depend on isms. The sound principle, he observed, in politics laid it down that no form of Government or political 'ism' was absolutely good or bad under all circumstances to all people alike. He, therefore, thinks it inadvisable to dictate to Germany, Japan, Italy or Russia to choose a particular form of Government. Democracy itself demands that the will of the people must prevail in choosing their own Government. Naturally he held that all those nations that were friendly or likely to be helpful to the Hindu Nation would be friends and allies of Hindustan.

To Savarkar, no academic and empty slogans of Democracy or Nazism or Fascism could be the guiding principle to India's foreign policy. He said we should never hate or love Fascists or Bolshevists or bookish reasons. There was no reason, he said, to suppose that Hitler was a human monster because he passed off as a Nazi or that Churchill was a demi-God because he called himself a democrat. Savarkar wanted Hindustan to maintain a policy of neutrality towards all nations in the world in respect of their internal affairs or mutual relations with each other. To him the ideal of Democracy and the ideal of Fascism made no difference. He measured the forces of liberty and freedom and the forces of Nazism and Fascism by the same standard. He had, it seems, no clearer and deeper conception of a new state; nor had he faith or interest in a new world order.

According to Savarkar, all nations look first to their own security and prosperity while dealing with international problems. They make or unmake pacts with this end alone in view. Let alone the history of pacts and treaties which Britain made with Indian Princes, whether great nations have stood by their pledges? By an agreement the USA was pledged to protect Korea. In 1905 Japan swallowed Korea and USA was the first nation to recognise the Korean conquest. The world knows the fate of Nine-Party Treaty of Brussels to stop Japanese Aggression. They orated and adjourned. The history of the Treaty of Rapallo, the Treaty of Berlin, the Treaty of 1933 and the dramatic end of the Non-Aggression Pact of 1939 between Germany and Russia is stunning and shocking.

Savarkar, however, said that the Hindu Mahasabha felt itself concerned with the issues at stake in the war so far as they were likely to affect the safety and interests of the Hindu Nation. He, therefore, appealed to the British Government to make an unambiguous declaration of granting Hindustan the status of a self-governing Dominion as an immediate step leading towards the final goal of complete independence and to introduce immediately responsible government at the centre based on the democratic principle of 'one man one vote'. He urged the Viceroy to guard India's Western Frontiers by High Schools and Colleges throughout India (as in England), to start and encourage rifle classes, to expand the Indian Territorial Force, to inspire the people of India to feel instinctively that the Indian Army was the Army of the people of India and not of Britain, and he appealed to the British Government not to use Indian forces outside India proper. Savarkar called upon Capital and Labour in the country to utilize the unique opportunity of the European War to capture the markets by working to capacity all the existing industries and by starting new ones and replacing at full speed all foreign articles by *Swadeshi*.

Out of fear and distrust the British rulers had kept India unarmed and unprepared. So the main object of Savarkar's war policy was to make Hindus re-animated and re-born into a martial race. It was in this belief that, like Tilak, he had supported from the Cellular Jail in the Andamans the militarization movement during World War I, and was delighted to hear that his countrymen were allowed to go to Europe in thousands to fight against the best military power in the world. In his youth, he wrote from London in 1906 quoting from the *Spectator* that soldiers could be thoroughly trained in six months, and casting a longing look at the then Boy Army of Britain, he felt that every Indian youth must learn Drill, Riding and Shooting. Long ago, in 1906 Savarkar observed in one of his letters from London that a nation's existence depended upon its political independence. If the nation enjoyed independence, it could make progress. That independence in its turn depended upon the mental and military training the nation imparted to its youth. That was why after his release the first slogan he raised was, "Down with the Arms Act, Start Rifle Classes."[13] Thus it can be seen from this that his militarization policy was consistent during both the World Wars.

Savarkar was the only all-India leader, and the Hindu Mahasabha was the only political Party in India that launched an intense propaganda for the militarization of the Hindus and for the industrialization of the country with pure patriotic and political objects during World War II. Long before the out break of World War II, Savarkar had seized every opportunity of bringing to the notice of the nation the woeful want of the military strength of the Hindus, whenever he spoke at schools and colleges and even at literary conferences. So he now wanted the youth to join the Army and to cross the seas to give fight and pass through the baptism of fire in all the world theatres of war and learn the use of the latest weapons.

Many people criticised Savarkar for his repeated emphasis on an increase in military might. Some of them even went to the length of branding him a Fascist. In fact, Savarkar's weakest point remained in his inability to distinguish between Democracy and Fascism. To him, the ideal of Democracy and the ideal of Fascism made no difference. He measured the forces of liberty and freedom and the forces of Nazism and Fascism by the same standard. He had, it seems no clearer and deeper conception of a new state; nor had he faith or interest in a new world order. Savarkar's sole obsession was to make Hindus re-animated and re-born into a martial race. However, Savarkar never, wanted to use violence without discrimination. He advised his compatriots to resort to violent means if and when other means failed to achieve the desired object. But the winds of unending questions never seem to stop: How could a backward country like India stand up against or be compared with England? Where were the arms in Hindustan? Was it possible even to think of facing the British artillery? Indian soldiers in the British army were most loyal to their Masters; then how could they be expected to rebel?

But Savarkar was ready with his answers: "Whose arms are those that are in the hands of the Indian soldiers? They are ours! Our Jawans may be uneducated but I am sure that the love of freedom resides in their hearts. Just try to make that light of freedom a little more lustrous and it will work wonders. Very soon you will see the same arms turning against the British. Savarkar was of the view that without the participation, or co-operation of the army it was impossible for any armed revolution to succeeded in bringing freedom to Hindustan."

Savarkar used to stress that the "Enemy's difficulty is our opportunity" and the "Enemy's enemy is our friend." This *'Mantra'* and his *'Tantra'* (of involving the Army in the struggle) were both like time-bombs kept under the very throne of the British Empire.[14] Moreover, till the day of Savarkar's whirlwind propaganda for Hindu militarization, military career was the monopoly of the Muslims, who formed the three-fourths of the Indian Army.[15] Both the Muslims and the British Government knew well what Savarkar's militarization movement stood for. It aimed at carrying politics into the military ranks of the Indian Army, and winning over the Army to the side of revolution for the final overthrow of the British yoke.

The ideal of Indian nationalism was in fact a noble one. The Hindus found nothing objectionable in the ideal of uniting all-India into a consolidated political unit and very naturally so, for it suited well with the Hindu mentality with its synthetic trend, always prone to philosophies with a universal urge. It is also true that the Ideal of Politics itself ought to be a Human state, all mankind for its citizens, the earth for its motherland. If the entire India with one-fifth of the human race could be united irrespective of religious, racial and cultural diversities, merging them all into a homogeneous whole, it would be but a gigantic stride taken by mankind towards the realisation of that human political ideal. The new concept of an Indian Nationality was founded on the only common bond of a territorial unity of India; the Hindus for one found nothing revolting even in that assumption to their deepest religious or cultural or racial sentiments. Because their national being had already been identified with that territorial unit, India, which to them was not only a land of sojourn but a home, their Father land, their Mother land, their Holy-land and all in one! Indian patriotism to them was but a synonym of Hindu patriotism. The British, too, while they favoured the Indian movement as an antidote to any possible revival of Hindu nationalism, took good care to see that the Moslem solidarity as Moslems did not suffer in any way by catching the contagion of this new Indian nationalist cult. For the British knew that if the Moslems also joined that cult as whole heartedly as the Hindus did, then there would really be a united Indian nation, a contingency likely to prove perhaps, more dangerous to British supremacy in India than a Hindu revival could single handedly prove to be.[16]

Thus, the policy of dividing Indians on communal lines (the notion of religion serving as the basis for the new political process based on popular participation) and giving support to the communalists became, from the end of the nineteenth century onwards, an important instrument of colonial policy in the effort to thwart the rising national movement. Virtually since the founding of the National Congress, parallel with its growth through different stages, and as an accompaniment to the process of constitutional reforms, the official policy of active promotion of communalism, was developed. This policy was also developed to meet the exigencies of politics back home in Britain where the growing democracy and labour movement were increasingly questioning imperialism in general and the policy of suppression of the popular national movement in particular.

Communalism was presented by the colonial administrators as the problem of the defence of minorities. And the defence of minorities became a major part of the theory of imperialist legitimation as its other components—welfare of the colonised, civilising mission, white man's burden—got increasingly discredited. The imperialist statesmen, officials and ideologues at that stage said that Britain had to continue to rule India because it alone could protect the minorities from domination, exploitation and suppression by the majority (The Indian, particularly the Muslim, communalist agreed and lent active support to this view).[17] The aim of the British policy of divide and rule was to check the politicization of the Indian people, to curb their consolidation and unification and to disrupt the process of the Indian nation-in-the-making. Once the anti-imperialist nationalist movement arose, the policy was also directed towards checking its growth, dividing its actual or potential supporters and preventing Muslims (as also landlords, capitalists, etc.) from joining it.

However, the official British commitment was not to communalism in itself but to its use for their own particular ends. The policy of divide and rule was not a perverse one. The aim was not to divide Indian society for its own sake or out of perversity or malice. It was not followed for itself or as a matter of principle but as a political instrument, and as a part of a broader political strategy of maintaining colonialism in the face of the nationalist challenge. For that reason, among others, it was used only to the extent needed. Similarly, its edges and contours were not the same throughout. It evolved gradually and changed to meet the changing times and the changing needs of colonial politics. It also differed from region to region. For example, it was not followed one-sidedly in Punjab as in

Bengal or U.P.; nor as actively between 1911 and 1923 as before 1911 and after 1930. The commitment to Muslim communalism became total only after 1939.[18] After 1937, the British had shifted from balanced to uncontrolled comn ınalism, encouraged total communal division, gave virtually open support to the Muslim League, especially in its anti-Congress role and tolerated its efforts to acquirc a mass character.[19]

As such, the first noticeable characteristic of Muslim political aggression, as Ambedkar pointed out 'Pakistan or the Partition of India', was their constantly increasing demand. The second thing was the spirit exploiting the weaknesses of the Hindus, like the Muslim's insistence upon cow slaughter and the stoppage of music before mosques. The third thing was the adoption by the Muslims of the 'gangster' method in politics. Dr. Ambedkar observed, "The riots are a sufficient indication that gangsterism has become a settled part of their strategy in politics."[20] On the other hand, the Congress policy was "to tolerate and appease the Muslims by political and other concessions.[21]

Here Ambedkar appears to be one with Savarkar in his analysis of the Hindu Muslim problem and in point holding the Congress squarely responsible for it. The policy of the Congress Party in power and in politics was entirely and grossly pro-Muslim. The rivalry of Hindu Mahasabha with the Congress had nothing to do with the issue of social reform *versus* political reform. Its quarrel with the Congress had its origin in the pro-Muslim policy of the Congress. Mahatma Gandhi never realised that this express attitude on his part was whetting Muslim appetite all the more. Even in 1931 he said, instead of bringing about *Swaraj* by force, it would be preferable to wait till the Congress became equally popular with the non-Hindus. This shows how far he had receded from reality. He had linked the future of the Hindus with the satisfaction of the Muslims. This was the danger that Savarkar realised. He held that accepting conditions of the Muslims for the sake of *Swaraj* was nothing less than slavery.

Frankly speaking, the Hindu Muslim problem had two aspects to it. In the first aspect, the problem that presented itself was the problem of two separate communities facing each other and seeking adjustment of their respective rights and privileges. In its other aspect, the problem was the problem of the reflex influences which that separation and conflict produced upon each of them.[22] As Savarkar had said, "As it is, there are two antagonistic nations living side-by-side in India, several infantile politicians commit the serious mistake in supposing that India is already welded into a harmonious nation, or that it could be welded thus for the mere wish to do so. These our well meaning but unthinking friends take their dreams for realities. But the solid fact is that the so-called communal questions are but a legacy handed down to us by centuries of a cultural, religious and national antagonism between the Hindus and the Moslems. When time is ripe you can solve them; but you cannot suppress them by merely refusing recognition of them."[23]

Savarkar also alleged that the India could not be assumed to be a unitarian and homogeneous nation, but on the contrary there were mainly two nations: the Hindus and the Moslems in India. He felt that the Hindus as a nation were willing to discharge their duty to a common Indian State on equal footing. But if the Muslims in India thrust on a communal strife on the Hindus and cherished anti-Indian and extra-territorial designs of establishing a Mohammedan Rule or supremacy in India then the Hindus would look to themselves and stand on their own legs and fight single handed as best as they can for the liberation of India from any non-Hindu yoke, be it English or Moslem or otherwise.

Savarkar believed that the Independence of India was in sight; but he sensed the danger to the integrity of India from the vacillating, servile, deceptive, and short sighted lead and policy of the Congress in respect of the blank cheque offers, the Communal Award (in 1932, the Government announced its decision on communal demands known as the Communal Award. The Award accepted all the major Muslim communal demands of the time. It guaranteed through reservations Muslim majority in Bengal and Punjab; it assured Muslims thirty-three and one-third per cent of the seats in the central legislature; it separated Sind from Bombay and introduced reforms in the North-West Frontier Province; and it decided to continue separate electorates. It was thus less an award than a pronounced favour shown to Muslim communalism. And it was based on an approach that fully accepted communal digits and the perpetual division of Indian political life on communal lines),"[24] the Simon Commission (with all non-Indian personnel to go into the question of constitutional reform), the census, the national script, the *lingua franca* and the national anthem.

In the meanwhile, the Muslim League Working Committee put forward its claim for a veto on all further political progress in the country on 18 September 1939 when it demanded that "no declaration regarding the question of constitutional advance for India should be made without the consent and approval of the All India Muslim League." It further demanded the ending of the federal scheme. It also claimed to be "the only organisation that can speak on behalf of Muslim India."[25] Jinnah and the League repeatedly reiterated the demand for a veto in the succeeding months, including at the famous Lahore Session in March 1940 where the demand for Pakistan was first put forward.[26] Commenting on Jinnah, Savarkar had asserted in 1938 in a press interview at Lahore that he and Jinnah were not birds of the same feather, because, while he stood for equality and no concessions, Jinnah did not stand for equality and always asked for more and more concessions. Savarkar told the press representatives that he insisted that either there should be joint electorates without any reservation of seats for any community in any legislature or any local body or there must be joint electorates with reservation of seats for minorities either on population basis or according to a system of weightages equally applicable to all minorities. He further said that the Congress should assume the role of a Parliament in which all parties should participate, and not the role of a party as it was developing in those days. A leading nationalist paper *Tribune* appreciated the services that Savarkar was rendering to the cause of the Motherland.

Savarkar's insight had perceived the growing danger from the designs of the awakened Muslim mind. He knew that Muslim opposition to the national aspirations was not confined to a song here or a piece of music there. According to him, there was a fundamental difference in their outlook on life and literature and in their aspirations for the governance of Hindustan as a nation. Therefore, the first thing Savarkar did was to strive to bring into operation the Federal part of the 1935 Act and frustrate the Muslim designs. Though the Federal part of this Act, he said, handed over no real power especially in the matter of military and foreign policy to the representatives of the people, it offered an opportunity for the realisation of national unification of the states and other parts under the British occupation into an organised and corporate whole.

The views of various parties and leaders on Pakistan differed. The Working Committee of the Congress passed a resolution at its Delhi Session in 1942 in which it declared that no territorial unit would be coerced into joining the Indian Union against its will. Gandhi and other Congress leaders, however, did not accept, in fact, combated the League's theory that the Indian Muslims form a nation. They rejected religion as the determinant of a nation, though recognising a group with a common religion as a cultural and communal minority.[27] Gandhi expressed to Louis Fischer, a well-known American journalist, his views: "We are not two nations... We in India have a common culture. In the North, Hindi and Urdu are understood by both Hindus and Moslems. In Madras, Hindus and Moslems speak Tamil, and in Bengal they both speak Bengali and neither Hindi or Urdu. When communal riots break out, they are always provoked by incidents over cows and by religious processions. That means that it is our superstitions that create the trouble and not our separate nationalities."[28]

In a letter to Jinnah in 1942, Gandhi wrote that he would have no objection to the British handing over power to the Muslim League on behalf of all Indians; the Congress would not only not oppose a government formed by the League on behalf of all Indians but would even participate in it, and clarified that he was saying this "in all seriousness and sincerity."[29] The Congress had no desire to force unity on the Muslims against their wishes. In 1940, Gandhi said, "We shall never take the help of the British to prevent partition. Muslims are free to impose their will on India either by themselves or with the help of the British."[30] However, Gandhi was convinced that if the Indian Muslims became determined to separate, no power could prevent them from doing so. He said, "I know no non-violent method of compelling the obedience of nine crores of Muslims to the will of the rest of India, however powerful a majority the rest may represent. The Muslims must have the same right of self-determination that the rest of India has. Any member may claim a division."[31]

The four years from 1943 to 1947 can be called the finest period of Savarkar's life. During this period, he organised a crusade single handedly to keep India united. The odds were against him. The Congress had a vice like grip on Hindu voters. And once the Congress resolve for a united India collapsed, it was impossible to raise a barrier against partition. There is no denying the fact that Savarkar strained every nerve to bring all forces interested in a united India together. He was of the opinion that "Indian Revolutionaries had a tough fight than the Revolutionaries in Russia or China. In Russia, they revolted against the Russian Czarist regime and in China against the Chinese Manchu dynasty. But in India we had to fight against foreign rulers, whose way of life, culture, religion and philosophy had nothing in common with the Hindus of Hindustan. In a way, our revolutionaries have been better than these revolutionaries of Russia and China."[32]

On 5 August 1944, he issued a common letter to the leaders of various parties making a proposal to hold Akhand Hindustan Leaders' Conference. Such a conference was held on 7 and 8 October in Delhi. It was presided over by Dr. Radha Kumud Mukherji. His Holiness Shankaracharya of Puri, Master Tara Singh, Sir Jogendra Singh and Dr. Khare, both members of the Viceroy's, Executive Council, Jamnadas Mehta, and 300 other leaders participated in it. In his closing address Savarkar said, "It is foolish to say that we Hindus cannot fight the British without the help of the Muslims. This imbecile attitude will help create Pakistan. Those who do not call themselves the sons of India are not our brothers but are our enemies."[33]

The joy of independence was almost delirious but lasted hardly 48 hours. Soon the news of communal troubles began to cast deep gloom. The whole of the Punjab, East and West, was becoming a graveyard of destruction and death. The magnitude of the carnage stunned all. The Policy inactivity cost thousands of lives during the communal killings of 1946-47. Both in Bengal and Punjab, officials from the highest to the lowest remained passive, inactive indifferent, irresolute and supine in the face of massive killings, butchery and one side pogroms, when elementary administrative integrity and activity could have saved thousands of lives. Since people could not get police protection during communal riots, they were forced to organize self-defence along Hindu or Muslim lines.[34]

And then history took an unexpected and different turn! In the midst of an atmosphere of extreme gloom, confusion and disaster, Nathuram Vinayak Godse shot Gandhi with a revolver while Gandhi was going to the prayer ground in the compound of Birla House, at Delhi in the evening at 5.30, on Friday, 30 January 1948, just five minutes after the talks Gandhi had with Sardar Patel for settling the differences between Patel and Nehru on the question of Muslim loyalty to India.

The reaction of this terrific act on the Hindu Mahaṣabha and the Rashtriya Swayamsevak Sangh was too severe and drastic, as the latter was regarded as a militant storm trooper offshoot of the Hindu Mahasabha. In his early youth, Godse was a worker of the R.S.S., and later he was a prominent member of the All India Committee of the Hindu Mahasabha. Furious crowds pulled down and burnt Hindu Sabha flags, destroyed local and district Hindu Sabha offices, burnt printing houses and studios belonging to the Hindu Sabha leaders, and attacked persons of Hindu Sabha persuasion, particularly persons from the caste of Godse. There was trouble and tension in a few cities between the Hindu Sabhaites and the R.S.S. on one side, and the violent crowds of Gandhian persuasion on the other.

In the first week of February about 25,000 Hindu Sanghatanists, including great and small men, were arrested. The R.S.S was outlawed. The government accused Savarkar of complicity in the deed and put him behind bars. The story of the prosecution was that Nathuram Godse was the tool, Apte the brain and Savarkar the Guru and guide behind the murder of Gandhi. The case was tried in the historic Red Fort at Delhi. Annasaheb Bhopatkar was the defence counsel of Savarkar. Others accused in the case, apart from Savarkar and Nathuram Godse, were Narayan D. Apte, Vishnu R. Karkare, Madanlal K. Pahwa, Shankar Kistaya, Gopal Godse and Dr. Parchure. The trial opened on 27

May 1948 and by mid-1949 Bhopatkar had conclusively proved Savarkar to be not guilty as there was no specific charge against him, and Justice Atmacharan had also ruled that Savarkar was to be set free as no guilt was attached to him. Thus, ended the Red Fort ordeal.

On his return to Bombay after the trial in Delhi, he again picked up the thread of his political life on 15 August 1949. He sent the following telegram to the President of the Constituent Assembly: "I am voicing the sense and sentiments of millions of our countrymen when I beseech the Constituent Assembly to adopt Bharat as the name of our nation, Hindi as the national language and *Nagari* as the national script."[35] Whoever may have been responsible, the Constituent Assembly chose the same things. In 1949, Savarkar went to Calcutta to inaugurate a session of the Hindu Mahasabha. In his speech, he emphasized one point: "Call it by whatever name you choose, call it Hindustan, Bharat, India or a Non-Muslim state, in the final analysis it remains a Hindu nation. And this for the simple reason that Hindus are in a majority. So long as this majority remains, the country will remain a Hindu nation."[36]

On 26 January 1950, when India became a Republic, Savarkar issued a statement just two days prior to the occasion, saying, "Let us sink our petty squabbles over provincialities, personalities and party platforms on that day and proclaim our national victory to the world. Let us first consolidate what we have already got and follow courageously the policy of tit for tat to all outsiders concerned and all will go well with us."[37]

The account thus is enough to prove that Savarkar was a true nationalist. He was an active political leader who either saw, talked or discussed Politics with thinkers from Ranade to M.N. Roy, leaders from Surendranath to Subhash Bose, from liberator Tilak to fighter Achyutrao Patwardhan! No other life on the political stage of India is marked by so many vicissitudes, punctuated with raging storms and lightening and tantalised with gaping gallows![38]

In his nationalistic fervour, Savarkar exhibited the spirit of Nanasahib, who fought the War of Indian Independence in 1857, the sweep of Wasudeo Balwant Phadke, who first raised an armed revolt in Maharashtra for the establishment of an Indian Republic, the mental force of Chiplunkar, the reformative zeal of Agarkar, the sacrifice and struggle of Tilak, the service of Gokhale and the untiring work of Kelkar. All these attributes find an echo in the alchemy of Savarkar. Savarkar proved to be a terror to tyrants, foe to injustice, an antidote to anti-nationalists and an unforging critic of the pro-Muslim politicians in India. And all in all, he was a unique combination of a dreamer and a doer, a prophet and a warrior, a realist and a revolutionary.[39]

Savarkar strove his utmost to avert the greatest betrayal in human history and the colossal disaster (the partition of the country), but was thwarted by the perfidy levity and betrayal of his contemporaries. But his contributions to our national struggle for freedom would not go unnoticed! In Savarkar's own words: "Some people say they won freedom without shedding a single drop of blood. True, very much true! Not even a single drop of blood has stained their creased clothes. But can we forget thousands of those tender boys and daring youths who, for freedom's sake, fell fighting in pools of their own blood?"[40]

REFERENCES

1. V.D. Savarkar, *Foreword to Hindu-Pad-Padshahi, op. cit.*
2. S.S. Savarkar and G.M. Joshi (eds.), *Historic Documents, V.D. Savarkar* (Bombay: Popular Prakashan), 1967.
3. V.D. Savarkar, *Hindutva, op. cit.*, p. 30.
4. *Ibid.*, p. 19.
5. *Ibid.*, p. 67.
6. *Ibid.*, p. 21.
7. *Ibid.*, p. 30.
8. Dhananjay Keer, *Veer Savarkar, op. cit.*, p. 273.
9. V.D. Savarkar, *Hindutva, op. cit.*, pp. 116-17.
10. *Ibid.*
11. V.D. Savarkar, *Hindu Rashtra Darshan, op. cit.*, p. 6.
12. V.D. Savarkar, Presidential Address at 19th Session of Akhil Bhartiya Hindu Mahasabha, *op. cit.*
13. Dhananjay Keer, *Veer Savarkar, op. cit.*, p. 252.
14. Shivaramu, *Savarkar's Role in British Quitting India*, Commemration Volume (Bombay: Savarkar Darshan Pratisthan), 1989.
15. Dhananjay Keer, *Veer Savarkar, op. cit.*, p. 257.

16. V.D. Savarkar, *Hindu Rashtra Darshan, op. cit.*, pp. 41-42.
17. Bipan Chandra, *Communalism in Modern India* (New Delhi: Vani Educational Books), 1984, p. 243.
18. *Ibid.*, pp. 245-246.
19. *Ibid.*, p. 256.
20. B.R. Ambedkar, *Pakistan or Partition of India* (Lahore: Mustaffa Waheed), 1976, p. 228.
21. *Ibid.*
22. *Ibid.*, p. 213.
23. V.D. Savarkar, *Hindu Rashtra Darshan, op. cit.*, p. 24.
24. Bipan Chandra, *Communalism in Modern India, op. cit.*, p. 269.
25. *Ibid.*, p. 272.
26. M.A. Jinnah, *Speeches and Writtings*, Vol. I (Lahore: Mustaffa Waheed), 1976, p. 89.
27. Bipan Chandra, *Communalism in Modern India, op. cit.*, p. 418.
28. D.G. Tendulkar, *Mahatma*, Vol. VI (New Delhi: Publications Division, Ministry of Information and Broadcasting, Government of India), 1958, pp. 93-103.
29. *Ibid.*, p. 48.
30. *Ibid.*, Vol. V, p. 269.
31. *Ibid.*
32. An excerpt from Savarkar's last press interview to Sridhar Telkar for the *Weekly Organiser*, Diwali, 1965 number.
33. S.M. Savarkar, and G. M. Joshi (eds.), *Historic Statements* V.D. Savarkar, *op. cit.*, pp. 130-133.
34. Bipan Chandra, *Communalism in Modern India, op. cit.*, p. 286.
35. S.M. Savarkar, and G.M. Joshi (eds.), *Historic Statements V.D. Savarkar, op. cit.*, p. 225.
36. *Ibid.*
37. *Ibid.*, pp. 227-229.
38. Jyoti Tehran, *Veer Savarkar Thought and Action of Vinayak Damodar Savarkar* (New Delhi: Deep and Deep), 1991, p. 86.
39. *Ibid.*
40. S.M. Savarkar, and G.M. Joshi (eds.), *Historic Statements V.D. Savarkar, op. cit.*, pp. 226-229.

6

RELATIVE NON-VIOLENCE

The peace and prosperity of the Hindus was the central aim of Savarkarian philosophy. To Savarkar what was conducive and whatever contributed to the human good was moral, justifiable, desirable and just. To him relative non-violence was a virtue and absolute non-violence was not only sinful, but immoral. Savarkar, therefore, hated the monomaniacal principle of absolute non-violence. A lioness besmeared with a deer's blood suckling her cubs at her breast was his nature's picture. He believed that man could not have saved himself from complete extinction had he not succeeded in adding strength of artificial arms to his natural arms. He said that the lesson was brawled on every page of history down to the latest page that nations which, other things equal, were superior in military strength survived, flourished and dominated while those which were militarily altogether weak were politically subjected or ceased to exist at all.

Hindu soul aimed at equality not only between human beings, but also equality amongst all beings. Therefore Hindustan preached and practised that strained water be given for horses and even corn throwing centres be opened in the oceans so that big fish should not swallow little ones. But while Buddhism was at its meridian, the Huns and the Scythians, came down like an avalanche upon India and trampled under their feet the Hindu families, their thrones, and their Gods. Pointing this to the Hindus, Savarkar said that the Holy-land of their love was devastated and sacked by hoards of barbarians, so inferior to them in language, religion, philosophy, mercy and all the soft and human attributes of man and God; but superior to them in strength alone; strength that summed up its creed, in two words—Fire and Sword! In trying to kill, killing India got killed and at last found that palm leaves at times are too fragile for steel. But during the days of Vikramaditya and Shalivahan valour accomplished what formulas had failed to do. Therefore, Savarkar concluded: "We denounce the doctrine of absolute non-violence not because we are less saintly, but because we are more sensible!"[1] The truth of this doctrine was demonstrated later in the measures adopted in Hyderabad, Kashmir and elsewhere.

Savarkar was one with great thinkers of the world. The controversy between the cult of absolute non-violence and the principle of relative non-violence is age long. All the saviours of humanity have supported the principle of relative non-violence. In Hindustan, Manu's immortal epigraphic command that an aggressor must be killed instantly, stands out distinctly. The great Shakespeare lays down that arms are fair when the intent of bearing them is just. Thomas Paine denounced the Quaker cult during the American War of Independence. "I am thus for a quaker," said Paine, "that I would gladly agree with all the world to lay aside the use of arms and settle matters by negotiation, but unless the whole world wills, the matter ends and I take my musket and thank heaven. He has put it in my power. . . We live not in a world of angels. The reign of Satan is not ended, neither can we expect to be defended by miracles." At another time he declared: "Wherefore, if you really preach from conscience and mean not to make a political hobby horse of your religion, convince the world thereby proclaiming your doctrine to our enemies for they likewise bear arms.... Preach repentance to your king and warn him of eternal ruin ... ye would not spend your invectives against the injured and insulted only, but like faithful ministers, cry aloud and spare none."[2] President Masaryk asked Tolstoy, the Russian apostle of the doctrine of absolute non-violence, as to why should a peace loving man void of evil intent be slain and not the man of evil purpose who killed.

Savarkar in his immortal work, "The Indian War of Independence of 1857", observed: "When Humanity will reach the goal of universal justice, of ultimate beatitude, when the millennium preached by the incarnations, by the *Messiahs*, and by religious preachers will be an accomplished fact on earth, when the resignation taught by Christ in the glorious words 'Whosoever shall smite thee on the right cheek, turn to him the other also' will be impracticable because, there will be no one to hit on the right cheek. In such a divine age, if anyone revolts, if anyone sheds a drop of blood, if anyone even whispers the word revenge, then at once, the sinner by this act, by his very utterance, would be eternally damned. For, when truth reigns in every heart, revolt must be a heinous sin. When everyone abhors killing, to shed a drop of blood must be a sin. In a time of such unchallenged Justice to punish a man even for uttering a sinful word would be altogether blameless."[3]

Savarkar continued in his rational approach to this problem: "But so long as that divine age has not arrived, so long as the highly auspicious end remains only in the lines of saintly poets and in the prophecies of the divinely inspired, and so long as, even to make that state of universal justice possible, the human mind has to be busy eradicating sinful and aggressive tendencies, so long, rebellion, bloodshed and revenge cannot be purely sinful."[4]

Savarkar believed that revolt, bloodshed and revenge had often been instrument created by nature to root out injustice and introduce an era of justice. He proceeded: "And when justice uses these terrible means for her salvation, the blame of it does not lie on justice but on the preceding cruel injustice, the power and insolence of which called forth the means. We do not hold the justice which gives the death sentence responsible for bloodshed, but rather the injustice which is taken to the gallows." Savarkar brilliantly concluded: "Therefore the sword of Brutus is holy. Therefore, the Waghanakh of Shivaji is sacred. Therefore, the bloodshed in the revolutions in Italy is of fair fame. Therefore, the beheading of Charles I is a just deed. Therefore, the arrow of William Tell is divine. And the sin of brutality falls heavily on the heads of those who committed the provoking injustice."[5]

Savarkar believed that had the world no fear of revolt, bloodshed and revenge, the earth would have bent under the devil-dance of unchecked robbery and oppression. "If oppression were to be secure," he observed, "from the fear that Nature would, sooner or later, create the avenger of temporary injustice, the whole world would have swarmed today with Tsars and Robbers! But because every Hiranyakashipu has his Narasimha; because every Dushshasana has his Bheema; because every evil doer has his avenger, there is still some hope in the heart of the world that injustice cannot last. Such a revenge, therefore, is nature's own reaction against injustice. And, therefore, the sin of the cruelty of that revenge rebound on the original evil doer."[6]

But in India when Savarkar was passing his days in internment her political leaders had made a hobby horse of the doctrine of non-violence and offered their advice to the insulted, enslaved and the butchered Hindus, supporting indirectly Nietzsche who believed that the resignation in Christianity was meant for the defeated and the downtrodden. This futile discussion and reiteration of this doctrine bankrupted the wit, baffled the brains, benumbed the revolutionary fervour, and seduced the hearts of the Hindus, softening their limbs and stiffening the bones of the enemies. Leader after leader blew hot and cold in the same breath while dealing with this doctrine. Some changed sides, abjured their faith, revoked their statements, and condemned their former patriotism and even previous life.[7]

Sarojini Naidu had been very vocal at the Lucknow session of the Indian National Congress in 1916: "It may seem a kind of paradox that I should be asked to raise my voice on, behalf of the dis-inherited manhood of the country, but it is suitable that I, who, represent the, other sex, that is, the mothers of the men whom we wish to make men and not emasculated machines, should raise a voice on behalf of the future mothers of India to demand that the birth-right of their sons should be given back to them, so that tomorrow's India may be once more worthy of its yesterday. ... The refusal of the privilege, that gifted privilege an inalienable right to carry arms, is to insult the very core of their valiant manhood!"[8]

Savarkars had a peculiar Maharashtrian approach. Even the great Maharashtrian saint, Tukaram, sings in a fit of practical righteousness: "Kill the scorpion, the despiser of the worship of God, if it enters the shrine; give tit for tat. No mercy to the wicked."[9]

Referring to absolute non-violence, Savarkar demanded it to be ruled out not only on practical but also on moral grounds. Savarkar's meeting with Subhas Chandra Bose on 29 June 1940 shaped his militarization policy well. There is no denying the fact that Savarkar was the main source of inspiration for the formation of the Indian National Army, whose founder Rasbehari Bose, an Indian revolutionary settled in Japan, was fully committed to Savarkar's mission of militarization and of armed revolution. It was Rasbehari who had informed Savarkar that Japan would enter the war before the end of the year 1940. Rasbehari even formed a unit of the Hindu Mahasabha in Japan after Savarkar became its President in 1937.[10] That was the time when Savarkar once again emerged on the active political scene after a lapse of 20 years.

Towards the middle of March 1941, the Liberal Circles held a Non-Party Conference at Bombay. The conference was convened by Tej Bahadur Sapru, and attended by intellectual luminaries of India, including Jagdish Prasad, Nripendranath Sirkar, Chimanlal Setalvad, Loknayak Aney, Moonje, Pandit Kunzru, Jayakar, Savarkar and Mookerjee.[11] Doubts regarding the representative character of the conference brought it to a crucial stage, but certain arguments given by Savarkar turned the course of events. Tej Bahadur Sapru expressed openly his gratitude to Savarkar and acknowledged that Savarkar's valuable guidance and spirit saved the conference from a debacle. It was at this conference that the Liberal leaders were indelibly impressed by Savarkar's intellectual and persuasive powers, and rational and realistic approach to the political problems. Even Srinivas Sastri was also quite impressed by Savarkar. Thus, Savarkar once again captivated the intellectual luminaries and lofty brains of India by his reason, intellect and the uncommon range and quality of his intellectual and argumentative powers. However, Jinnah declared that the conference was engineered by the agents of the Congress and the Hindu Mahasabha.

The 23rd Annual Session of the Hindu Mahasabha to be held at Bhagalpur in 1941 was banned by the Government. The Government justified the ban with unabashed frankness by stating that they had to do so for no other urgent or, justifiable reason, but to enable the Bakr-Id festivities of a handful of Moslems in a solitary town like Bhagalpur to pass off well."[12] Savarkar reacted, "It is only the insane policy of the Government to placate Moslem goondaism that has rendered the Moslem fanatics so irascible and intolerant." The Mahasabha, however, consequently resolved to hold its session at Bhagalpur itself on the scheduled dates inspite of the unjust, humiliating and illegal government ban, in assertion of the civic rights of citizenship in general and of Hindus in particular. "We go to Bhagalpur not to challenge the government but to assert our legitimate rights."[13] So thousands of Hindu Mahasabha volunteers defied the ban and tried to hold the session. They were arrested and released after about a week.

This resistance movement was so powerful that it did not need the support of any party or leader. The session was held in Bhagalpur, when G.V. Ketkar, with the rebellious spirit of his grand-father, Lokmanya Tilak, rose to the occasion and read out Savarkar's presidential address, who was arrested at Gaya en route to Bhagalpur and put in jail.

The Bhagalpur Civil Resistance success proved to be a source of strength and self-confidence, and demonstrated that inspite of castes, creeds, sects and sections, Hindus did pulsate with a common national urge, proving that Pan-Hindu consciousness was a vigorous reality. However, the first successful manifestation of Pan-Hinduism under the leadership of Savarkar was heralded way back in 1938 in Hyderabad (Bhaganagar as it was known before its conquest by the Muslims). The struggle to wrest some basic civil liberties and political rights for the Hindu majority of the Hyderabad state, organised by Savarkar in 1938, laid the foundation stone of its liberation in 1968. Savarkar's mission was finally and successfully completed by Sardar Patel.

Never before the Hindus united so successfully for a political struggle. Under the leadership of Savarkar, Hindus of all castes and creeds Sanatanis, Arya Samajists—compelled the Nizam to grant basic civil liberties and political rights to his Hindu subjects. For centuries, the Nizam ruthlessly followed the policy of Islamization of his Hindu subjects by denying them positions of power to match with their overwhelming numerical majority. The Hindus and the Sikhs in the State were not allowed to hold meetings, take out processions, political or religious, renovate their temples, or to start even private schools to educate the children in their mother tongue. Hindu temples, Hindu Bazars and Hindu houses were burnt down;

12 per cent Muslim population held 80 per cent posts, positions and jobs of vantage in the administration.[14]

Describing the Nizam's opposition to the Civil Resistance Movement at the 21st Session of Hindu Mahasabha in Calcutta in 1939, Savarkar thundered, "For this *Dharma Yuddha,* this fight for the righteous Hindu cause proved to demonstrate that inspite of caste and creeds, sects and sections, Hindudom as a whole does still pulsate with a common National Being."[15]

The struggle also included the formation of the *Hindu Civil Liberties Union* (which was almost an offshoot of the Hindu Mahasabha) by the Hindu subjects of the Hyderabad State under the leadership of Veer Yashwantrao Joshi; the launching of one-man civil disobedience movement against the Nizam's atrocities over his Hindu subjects, by Senapati Bapat, Savarkar's colleague during his revolutionary activities in Great Britain who later on joined the Indian National Congress; the participation of many activists of the Rashtriya Swayamsevak Sangh under the banner of the Hindu Mahasabha (of course, in their individual capacity) and the participation by several hundred Sikh volunteers from Punjab who were inspired by Master Tara Singh, the President of Shri Gurudwara Prabandhak Committee. It may be referred here that Savarkar had met Master Tara Singh in 1938 at the famous Golden Temple in Amritsar. Personally, Savarkar toured Maharashtra, Delhi, Punjab, Bihar and Bengal, and made appeals to the Hindus to intensify the struggle against the despotic Nizam. The struggle was not a bed of roses. Thousands had to suffer the brutalities of the Nizam's administration. But the victory was knocking at the door steps!

This successful termination of the struggle for the civic, political, economic and religious rights of the Hindus and Sikhs, who were totally suppressed in the Hyderabad State, was a new feather in Savarkar's cap, and added prestige and power to his leadership. Hyderabad struggle was the first successful civil disobedience Movement in the history of modern India. It was the first successful political manifestation of Pan-Hinduism. It was the first victory of the Hindus over the Muslims in the latter's bastion in modern India. It revealed the unique leadership qualities, organisational skills, political acumen and missionary zeal of Savarkar.

Hence it is evident from the foregoing account of his life, activities and policies that Savarkar is no believer in the doctrine of non-violence. To him relative non-violence is a virtue. The lesson of history is that other things being equal, nations which are superior in military strength flourish and dominate, while those which are militarily weak go down before others and become subject to foreign rule. When Buddhism was the dominating faith in India, she fell easy victim to the Huns and the Shakas who trampled under their feet Hindu temples and Hindu Kingdoms. He is one of the few leaders who deliberately opted for the policy of militarizing the Hindus with a view to making them into a martial race. During the World War II, he advised the Hindus to join the military, navy and air force in large numbers because that gave them best opportunity of acquiring training in the use of modern arms. Even before the outbreak of the War, he drew the attention of the Hindus so far as military training was concerned.

REFERENCES

1. Dhananjay Keer, *Veer Savarkar, op. cit.*, p. 275.
2. Some of Paine's Masterpieces (New York: Watts & Co.), 1960, p. 273.
3. V.D. Savarkar, *Indian War of Independence, op. cit.*, p. 273.
4. *Ibid.*
5. *Ibid.*, p. 274.
6. *Ibid.*
7. Dhananjay Keer, *Veer Savarkar, op. cit.*, p. 277.
8. Sarojini Naidu *Speeches and Writings* (Madras: G. A. Natesan & Co.), 1945, p. 78.
9. Dhananjay Keer, *Veer Savarkar, op. cit.*, p. 279.
10. *Ibid.*, p. 260.
11. *Ibid.*, p. 290.
12. V.D. Savarkar, *Hindu Rashtra Darshan, op. cit.*, p. 172.
13. *Ibid.*
14. *Veer Savarkar: The Crusader of Bhaganagar Freedom Struggle, Commemoration* Volume, *op. cit.*
15. O.P. Rehlan (ed.), *Hindu Mahasabha*, Vol. II (New Delhi: Anmol), 1997, p. 440.

7

REVOLUTION

In all great religious and political revolutions, it is almost impossible to connect together links apparently inconsistent, without thoroughly understanding principles which are at their root. On seeing a great work of machinery composed of innumerable screws and wheels doing work of tremendous magnitude, if we do not understand how the power is produced, we may feel bewildering astonishment, but never the inner pleasure due to knowledge. When writers describe such stirring events as the French Revolution or the religious revolution of Holland, the very splendour and magnitude of the crises they paint, often, dazzle and confuse their mind's eye and they rarely gather sufficient coolness and courage to go deep into the underlying principles. But without an exposition of the hidden causes and the mysterious forces that worked beneath, the essence of a revolution can never be made plain. And therefore it is history that attaches more importance to the exposition of principles than mere narrative.

While searching for principles, historians often commit another mistake. For every act, there are various causes, direct and indirect, general and particular, accidental and necessary. In their proper classification lies the true skill of the historian. In this process of classification many historians get mixed up and make the accidental into a necessary cause. This leads to an error, for example, the judge in the story who, in a case of arson, put all the responsibility on the 'match' instead of the 'man' who struck it. The real importance of any event can never be understood by this confusion of causes. Not merely that, but mankind begins positively to curse the memory of men who are represented as having started, with a light heart and private selfish motives, a Revolution in the course of which countless lives are lost and immense expanses of country devastated. And therefore, in writing the history of any event in general, and of revolutionary movements in particular, a writer cannot give a true idea of them by means of simple description, or even by tracing them backwards to accidental causes. An upright and impartial historian must try to discover the foundations on which the revolutionary structure was erected. He must try to discover and discuss fundamental causes.

Mazzini, in a critical article on Carlyle's *French Revolution*, has said that every revolution must have had a fundamental principle. Revolution is a complete re-arrangement in the life of historic man. A revolutionary movement cannot be based on a flimsy and momentary grievance. It is always due to some all moving principle for which hundreds and thousands of men fight, before which thrones totter, crowns are destroyed and created, existing ideals are shattered and new ideals break forth, and for the sake of which vast masses of people think lightly of shedding sacred human blood. The moving spirits of revolutions are deemed holy or unholy in proportion as the principle underlying them is beneficial or wicked. As in private life, so also in history, the deeds of an individual or a nation are judged by the character of the motive. If we forget this test, we cannot appreciate the vast difference between the empire building wars of Alexander the Great and Italy's fight for liberty under Garibaldi. Just as to decide about the merits of these two different events one has to consider the prime motive of the chief actors in those wars, so also to write a full history of a revolution means necessarily the tracing of all the events of that revolution back to their source, the motive, the innermost desire of those who brought it about. This is the telescope which will show clearly the lights and shadows obscured by the blurred presentation, of partial and prejudiced historians. When a beginning is made in this manner, order appears in the apparent chaos of inconsistent facts, crooked lines become straight, and straight lines appear crooked, light appears where darkness is, and darkness spreads over light, what appeared ugly becomes fair and what looked beautiful is seen to be deformed.

And expectedly or unexpectedly, but in a clear form, the Revolution comes into the light of real history.[1]

The history of the tremendous Revolution that was enacted in India in the year 1857 has never been written in this specific spirit by any author, Indian or foreign. And hence we witness throughout the world most extraordinary, misleading, and unjust ideas about a Revolutionary War. English authors have committed, in this respect, all the faults noted above. 'Some of them have not made any attempt beyond merely describing the events, but most of them have written the history in a wicked and partial spirit. Their prejudiced eye could not or would not see the root principle of that Revolution. Is it possible that an all embracing Revolution could have taken place without any objective or principle behind it ? Could that vast tidal wave from Peshawar to Calcutta have risen in flood without a fixed intention of drowning something by means of its force? Could it be possible for the sieges of Delhi, the massacres of Cawnpore, to take place without a noble and inspiring end? Even a small village market is not set up without an end, a motive. Thus how can we believe that the great market opened and closed without any purpose—the great market whose shops were on every battle field, from Peshawar to Calcutta, where kingdoms and empires were being exchanged, and where the only current coin was blood. The market was neither opened nor closed without a purpose. English historians have always ignored this point, not because it is difficult to ascertain, but because it is against their interests to admit the truth.[2]

Revolution: Why and How?

"A revolution is evolution in leaps."[3] Further: "Revolutions are not regulated by fixed laws. They are not accurately working machines like clocks and watches. They have their own way of marching. They can only be regulated by a general principle; but they brush away minor rules by their very shock. Revolution has only one watchword—Dash on. All sorts of new and unthought of circumstances might arise during its progress; but one must stop, one must overcome them and press forward"[4], wrote Savarkar.

According to Savarkar, indecision and delay mar a revolution: "There is no other life-killing poison to a revolution than indecision. The sooner and the more sudden the spreading of a revolution, the greater are its chances of success. If delay is made after the first start and breathing time is given, the enemy gets time to guard himself; those who rise prematurely lose confidence, when they see no one joining them; and a clever enemy, profiting by the past, puts obstacles in the way of those who want to rise later. Therefore, to give the enemy time between the first rising and the spreading of a revolution is always harmful to the revolution."[5]

Every revolution is started by cutting down the laws of existing authority by the sword. However, once the habit of moving down by the sword the unjust laws of unconstitutional authority is formed, then in the heat of moment, the vicious habit of negating all laws at will becomes the general norm. The sword used for destroying wicked and cruel laws tends to destroy all laws, including the good ones. The heroes, who start out for overthrowing foreign rule, soon get into the habit of overthrowing all rule. In the excitement of breaking the bonds of foreign rule, they begin to dislike all bonds even those of just and normal rule. And in this way, revolution ends in an anarchy, virtue in vice, and what ought to be a great benefit ends in loss.

"The destruction of individuals, of society and of Kingdoms is caused as much by anarchy as by foreign rule, as much by the absence of any bond as the presence of cruel bonds. If any revolution forgets this sociological truth it generally kills itself in the end. Just as a man who begins to take wine as a cure for some distemper does not get rid of the habit of drinking wine even after he is secured, similarly the habit of breaking bonds in order to remove bad rule, persist even after its work is done and makes men disorderly and anarchical. That revolution which destroys injustice and oppression is holy. But when a revolution roots out one kind of injustice and oppression and plants, at the same moment the seeds of another kind, it becomes at once unholy and the seeds of destruction accompanying that sin soon put an end to its life.[6]

Therefore, those who want to take the wine of revolution to cure the disease of foreign slavery must be on their guard and not get addicted. The mind must be trained from the beginning to honour one's own rule as much as to hate foreign rule. In wiping out foreign misrule, care must be taken to discourage, by all possible means, internal disorder. In smiting down foreign rule and foreign authority, one's own rule and authority should be worshiped as sacred. The moment the foreign power is destroyed, in order to guard the country from the evils of anarchy, a constitution favoured by the majority of the people should be at once established and that constitution should be obeyed with reverence by all. The orders of all officers thus appointed must be implicitly carried out, discipline must be observed, individual caprice must give the way to devotion to the principle of common good and if any change in any constitution is thought desirable and just, it must be attempted only by means of the voice of the majority. In short, the rule should be revolution outside and constitution within, chaos outside and cosmos within, sword outside and law within."[7]

Social Revolution

With his internment in Ratnagiri, after return from the Andamans, Savarkar himself took up the task of social revolution. On 6 January 1924, the *Ratnagiri Hindu Sabha* was established ostensibly through the influence and attempts of Babarao Savarkar, the elder brother of Veer Savarkar, but, infact, inspired by Savarkar himself.[8] He took two major activities in hand, reconversion and removal of untouchability. He gave his first speech on 'Untouchability and the Reconversion Movement' at Parsuram on 17 April 1924. About a year later, one Mahadev Laxman Gurav decided to install an idol in the Hanuman temple and requested Savarkar to be chief guest. Savarkar convinced Gurav of the importance of removal of untouchability. So, at the time of the function, the *palanquin* was carried by Mahars, Mangs, Chamars, Brahmins and Marathas. For this function, Savarkar composed a stirring poem titled, "We Hindus are all brothers of each other." The first reconversion at Savarkar's instance took place in 1925, when one Jadhav, who had become a Christian, was brought back to the Hindu fold. The next year a whole Brahmin family, converted to Christianity, was reconverted.

In 1930, the orthodox section of Brahmins decided to sabotage the growing campaign against untouchability. They passed a resolution that untouchables would not be permitted to enter the Vithal Mandir during the Ganapati festival. Savarkar countered this move by having a separate Ganapati festival for all Hindus. The idol was installed and worshipped by one Shiva Bhangi. The prize for reciting the *Gayatri Manatra* was also won by a Bhangi boy. However, the crowning achievement of the anti-untouchability movement was the raising of the *Patit Pavan Mandir* for all Hindus. Orthodox sections opposed the installation of the idol with Vedic rites by Bhagojiseth Keer, who was a Bhandari by caste. Savarkar contended that Vedic rites could be performed by a Mahar or a Maharaja, but when he found that the local orthodox section was bent on opposition he called learned Bhramins, sympathetic to his views, from outside and the idol was installed at the hands of Bhagojiseth.

In the meanwhile, the independent movement started by Ambedkar in 1924 for the liberation of the untouchables also came to a head. It hated the sense of dependency and abhorred the feeling of patronage of caste Hindu reformers. "Tell the slave he is a slave and he will revolt", was its slogan. Self-elevation and the self-help was the symbol on its standards. Ambedkar unfurled the banner of revolt at Mahad in December 1927.[9] Savarkar was one of those who fearlessly and whole-heartedly supported Ambedkar's struggle.

Upholding that struggle for human rights, Savarkar said that untouchability must be condemned and abolished not only as the need of the hour but also the command of the true religion; not only as a policy or as an act of expediency but also as a matter of justice; not only as a matter of obligation but also as a service to humanity. He, therefore, declared that the pious and bounden duty of the Hindu world at large was to restore full human rights to their co-religionists. Savarkar's teachings and message to the untouchables were appealing. He asked them to live a simple life, and to shed their inherent inferiority complex. He admonished them that for their own welfare they should suffer with fortitude and faith. He asked them not to abandon their occupations but to stick to them and improve them because every occupation had its value.

He also preached them for never disowning their fathers, saints and blood.[10]

Savarkar's social thought also constituted his relentless criticism against socially harmful age old Hindu customs, traditions, practices and beliefs with special emphasis on the abolition of caste. Caste based on birth is a unique feature of the Hindu social structure justified by *Shruti* and *Saruti*. It has far-reaching serious consequences. John Gunther has rightly observed, "Caste determines religious, social, economic and domestic life from cradle to grave." However, Savarkar totally rejected the view that caste is determined by birth. He argued that originally the caste system was based on the virtues and work of individuals. The caste system aimed at division of work in the Hindu society. In course of time, the Hindu social structure began to degenerate and a rigid caste system based on birth prevailed in practice. Customs and traditions of castes are described by Savarkar as the seven chains that enslave Hindu society. Restrictions on reading of *Vedas,* inter-caste dinning, inter-caste marriages, occupational freedom, sea voyages and reconversion of converted Hindus are the six chains, while untouchability is the seventh chain. Hindus should break the chains and get themselves liberated.[11]

The question of temple entry for the Untouchables cropped up in 1925. The orthodox quarters were alarmed. They shouted that their religion, God and traditions were in danger. Their religion and traditions and customs welcomed an Untouchable provided he became a Mohammad or a Minto. The orthodox who touched animals like bullocks and buffaloes, could endure the presence of a dog or a cat in their houses, but not the presence of their co-religionist Hindu *Mahars* or Hindu *Bhangis* though they were human beings! They feared that their sacred God would be polluted by the mere sight of a Hindu *Bhangi.* 'He is not God who can be desecrated', went the epigrammatic Savarkarian reply to the orthodox. Savarkar held that those men who regarded such inhuman faith as abhorred on the touch of a human being and yet gladly touched animals like dogs and cats, were themselves a blot on humanity. It was they who were really fallen and not the 'untouchables'! Removal of untouchability, he added, therefore, implied purification and invitation of such misguided orthodox touchables also!

Orthodoxy began to collapse under such ruthless arguments. To pull down the steel walls of orthodoxy, Savarkar started Pan-Hindu Ganesh festivals in 1925. He transformed the Ganesh Festival started by Tilak into a Pan-Hindu festival. An Untouchable was not allowed for ages within the precincts of the Hindu sanctuaries. Gradually, the question of temple entry was discussed with wisdom and vehemence during the days of Ganesh festival. The untouchables were brought into the hall of the Vithoba temple, the most important temple in Ratnagiri District.

Savarkar's propaganda was not one-sided. With a batch of his workers, he visited the slums and squalid dens, hamlets and hills, villages and towns where the Untouchables lived. This batch studied their ways of living, taught them cleanliness, guided them, and worshipped with them. They took the *Chamars* into the quarters and temples of the *Mahars* and the *Bhangis* into the quarters and temples of the *Dhors*.

Another battle on the home front as such Savarkar had with the Hindu orthodoxy or the Sanatanists was over the question of mixed caste schools in the district. The orthodox Hindus opposed the idea tooth and nail. The School Board faltered and the District Board failed in its support.

So Savarkar carried on intense propaganda in favour of mixed schools through the press and from the platform and appealed to the district and provincial authorities for help against the forces of orthodoxy which denied the just, civic, human, and legitimate rights to the children of the untouchables to sit in public schools along with the caste Hindu children. Attention of the Government also was drawn by Savarkar to the fact that the untouchables being as good tax-payers and citizens as the touchables, their children were entitled to the benefit of all public schools. It was also pointed out that those very orthodox Hindus did not feel any qualms of conscience in allowing the Christian and Muslim children to sit by their children in schools.

Savarkar appealed to the orthodox Hindus not to treat their co-religionists like dogs and cats. "Can you prevent Christian children from attending public schools? No. You dare not. You know the consequences. The British Government will speak with bullets," he challenged. "You insult the Untouchables, because they are ignorant and helpless; but you yield to the unjust demands of the Muslims because they are aggressive. When a *Mahar* becomes a Muslim or a Christian convert, you treat him as your equal. But as a *Mahar* he will not receive the same treatment. What a shame my countrymen!" he thundered.[12]

The discussions and debates with opponents over the burning problem of reconversion and Hindu Organisation continued. Stirring speeches and moving appeals would go on till early dawn. The next morning saw Savarkar in another village and this way his propaganda went on. Savarkar was then in the best of his health. Men of wealth, distinction and status followed him climbing hills and dales with cheer. The suppressed people watched and waited for his arrival at their villages with bewilderment and hope and crowded for the *darshan* of Savarkar, the saviour of the fallen Hindus, who opened to them the gates of the temples of God, Man and Light.

Savarkar's outlook was absolutely modern and secular. He showed the fallacy and hollowness of time worn and scripture born arguments. He denounced the ideologies that described the machine as a device of the devil invented to spite the glory of God and to strike a blow at the influence of religion and make man feeble, mechanical, helpless and heartless, leading him to his final doom. Savarkar ruthlessly exposed this false propaganda. So he was to Maharashtra what eighteenth century great European reformers were to Europe.

About the God of Man and the Lord of the universe, Savarkar had peculiar views. According to him, we live in this world, but the universe has nothing to do with us. The belief that what the Lord of the universe likes is good and what He likes must be beneficial to the progress of Man, is useless, because it is not true. The forces in the universe are to a little degree for Man, but to a greater extent they are against him. What man can do at the most is to learn the laws of the universe as best as he can, and turn them to his benefit and welfare. This is, he sums up, the real worship of the universe.

In his view, whatever contributes to human good is good, what is derogatory to the progress of humanity is bad. The definition of morality should be framed, he says, in reference to the common good of mankind. If God is kind enough to take a man out of danger, and is all pervading, who first throws a virtuous man into the flames of danger, he asks. Who sinks steamers full of men, children and women despite heartfelt prayers? Who sets a conflagration to the woods and roasts the birds, reptiles and other creatures like fish? Savarkar asks: 'Why does God make the wicked so powerful as to be in a position to harass the good? If God is omniscient and most kind, does he not know the innocence and purity of that good man beforehand? Why does he at all test the virtuous man through cruel and fierce ordeals?' In this respect Savarkar is more agnostic than Ingersoll, and more balanced than Agarkar, the giant rationalist of Maharashtra.[13]

Savarkar feels sorry that superstition should hold its sway in our land even during the twentieth century. "We have allowed the Britishers to crush everything that was with us, but not that precious possession of ours, our credulous superstitions! Let an earthquake occur, public prayer is our remedy. Let a patriot fall ill, we go to attend a crowded prayer meeting. Let a pestilence ravage our land, and we kill goats in sacrifice to ward off the calamity. It was quite all right when we did not know the causes of such things, but to stick to these superstitions even when science has revealed the causes of such calamities is simply absurd." writes Savarkar.[14]

Savarkar asks the Hindus to follow the cause and effect theory that is never disturbed by the thought of Divine pleasure or displeasure. He points out to the people that water boils at a certain temperature and God never interferes in this process. Oxygen and Hydrogen combined in proper proportions, are bound to yield water any day of the year whether God wills it or not! He proceeds: "With the aid of science, even Godless Russia is actually floating castles in the air in the form of aeroplanes and giant super-fortresses." "What actually matters is scientific accuracy and not astrological superstition. Astrology cannot save what science has doomed and where safety is assured by science, astrology cannot endanger it," he observes, in his brilliant article entitled, 'Machine is a boon to Mankind.'[15]

Savarkar tells the people that it is time for them to realize that 'sacrifice' cannot bring rains, nor can it avert a famine. He appeals to the Hindus to discard the superstitions and religious aspect clinging to their usages regarding maternity and asks them to send their women to well-equipped, well-lighted, modern maternity homes instead of galling them in dark, dingy and smoky rooms. He suggests that the corpses should be carried in a car in a decent manner and burnt in electric crematorium.

"Machine has made it possible for man stay to beneath water, rise high up in the sky. Machine has made man far-reaching, far-seeing, far-speaking and far-hearing. Machine has conferred upon man blessings which no prophets could give or no penance could secure. Mankind owes its present civilization entirely to the use of machine, and thus machine far from being a curse, is a wonderful boon which has bestowed supernatural powers upon this human race!", observes Savarkar. He appeals to the nation that it is the duty of every thinking man to promote the principles of science in every department of life. Without it, no nation can hope to survive the present stage, he adds.

To Savarkar science by itself is not responsible for the evils of capitalism or the destructive orgy of modern war technique. It is the fault of the ways of distribution, lust for domination, and greed for exploitation. Electricity can light a bulb or detonate a bomb for the destruction of a city. Sarvarkar says that the evil should be checked. In short, he observes, not warfare but welfare of mankind should be the ultimate goal of science.

Savarkar stands for science and absolute science. He stands for today and not for the blind traditions of yesterday. He appeals to the Hindus to test all their ancient holy works on the touchstone of science. He writes: "We do not regard the ancient works as all pervading, omniscient and perfect by themselves. The *Smritis* and the *Vedas* we love reverentially, not as omniscient and unchangeable works, but as historical books and as the land marks in the great and glorious journey of the human race. "He, therefore, asks the Hindus to test the knowledge in the ancient holy works, their laws and learnings on the touchstone of science and to follow fearlessly what contributes to the good of the nation.

To Savarkar, no animal is sacred. Even the cow is meant for man; not man for the cow. There should be cow-worship but not cow protection. He denounces the viewpoint of the Hindu leaders of the past, who, for saving the lives of a handful of cows, lost their kingdoms, their human rights, and their all. He, therefore, observes that if it is inevitable in a grave crisis to live upon beef and save human lives in India, the Hindus should also do it. The prosperity of a nation does not depend upon its capacity for penance and yoga but on, love of justice, or sense of virtue. History is replete with innumerable instances, he writes, which show that the wicked, cruel, unjust and inhuman kings, conquerors, democracies and republics have smothered the weak kings and powerless democracies, though the victims were just, human and non-aggressive. Discipline dry gunpowder, the range of guns, the sharp edge of swords and an unflinching will are the factors that protect the rights and liberties of a nation. Justice and injustice have no relation to victory or defeat. Victory and defeat are quite different from justice and injustice. If victory and defeat have at any relation with any other thing, it is valour, observes Savarkar. But this worship of strength, power and discipline, Savarkar says, should not be used for aggressive and greedy aims. He states that justice, if weak, is futile and lame. It goes under. Injustice, if powerful, tramples upon it.

As for the role of women in life, Savarkar has definite views to offer. He believes that there is a fundamental and natural difference between man and woman. Their duties are different. So their education, too, must necessarily differ. Reformer as he is, he does not like women to obey the dictates of old useless customs.

Savarkar regards female education indispensable to the uplift of a nation; but by female education he does not necessarily mean university degrees, although he has no objection to their obtaining the degrees without disregarding their primary duty to the home, children, and the nation. He holds that a system of education must be drawn up on new lines, and women should be given some sort of specialized training congenial to the temperament of women. A woman should be a ministering angel rather than a masculine

Amazon or a Virago. She should imbibe the quality of her proverbial modesty and grace rather than mere eloquence or proficiency in mathematics. Women are the solace and comfort of hearths and homes. The larger the number of good healthy mothers, he observes, the stronger and healthier will be the nation. Therefore, a woman's education should enable her to enrich the nation with a generation stronger, more beautiful, and more patriotic than the past. The Russian woman is on an equal footing with man. Yet, does it mean, he asks, that a Stalin delivers a child instead of his wife?[16]

To Savarkar life is an oblation. According to him, a woman should look beautiful with her natural charms and try to keep it with good aids to beauty. In addition, he has something to say to a beauty about her duty. Beauty is handed over to her, he warns, as a strict sacred trust. And that trust is eugenics. A beautiful woman who fails to fulfil this condition becomes morally guilty of a breach of trust. A nation that strives to have daughters more beautiful than their mothers and sons stronger than their fathers necessarily adds to artistic culture handed down to it through heritage. Is this not the angle and approach of a realist and a reformer? Years after Savarkar wrote this, we find today England, France and other European countries propagating these very doctrines to arrest the decrease in population in their countries and to avoid the consequential downfall and decay of the virility of their nations.

Even at the risk of being branded as a communalist, Savarkar always liked to be a realist rather than a man of clouds. Infact, in the domain of realism, rationalism and revolutionism, Savarkar seemed to surpass many of his contemporaries.

Savarkar was fully aware of the strength and weakness of the ancient Hindu culture and civilization. Even though he wanted the Hindus to look forward to the West for its achievements in the field of science and technology, he did not want them to be oblivious of their glorious past. He interpreted Indian history with a view to throwing light on the unparalleled achievements of Hindus in different areas of life. Hindus could march forward with confidence if they properly realise the achievements of their forefathers. Savarkar felt that the Hindus should derive inspiration from the glorious past and make themselves one of the most powerful and progressive nations of the world by adopting the new way of life. Thus, it is true that Savarkar's social thinking was based on social equality, sense of justice and intellectualism.

REFERENCES

1. V.D. Savarkar, *The Indian War of Independence*, 1857, *op. cit.*, p. 3.
2. *Ibid.*, p. 4.
3. *Ibid.*, p. 159.
4. *Ibid.*
5. *Ibid.*, p. 128.
6. *Ibid.*
7. *Ibid.*
8. Dhananjay Keer, *Veer Savarkar, op. cit.*, p. 167.
9. *Ibid.*, p. 182.
10. *Ibid.*, pp. 188-89.
11. S.N. Navalgundkar, *Hindus Unite, Modernise and Militarize*, Commemoration Volume, *op. cit.*
12. Dhananjay Keer, *Veer Savarkar, op. cit.*, p. 178.
13. *Ibid.*, p. 204.
14. *Ibid.*
15. *Ibid.*, p. 205.
16. *Ibid.*, p. 213.

8

SAVARKAR'S INDIA

Dhanajay Keer, the celebrated author of 'Veer Savarkar' and a biography of Savarkar, made a blue print of Savarkar's India. He discussed the draft with Savarkar himself, who made some changes. The final draft reads as under:

I

1. In Savarkar's India all citizens would have equal rights and obligations irrespective of caste, creed, race or religion, provided they avow and owe an exclusive and devoted allegiance to the State.
2. All minorities would be given effective safeguards to protect their language, religion, culture, etc. but none of them would be allowed to create a State within a State or to encroach upon the legitimate rights of the majority.
3. The fundamental rights of freedom of speech, freedom of conscience, of worship, of association, etc. would be enjoyed by all citizens alike; whatever restrictions would be imposed on them in the interest of the public peace and order or national emergency would not be based on any religious or racial considerations alone but common national grounds.
4. 'One man one vote' would be the general rule irrespective of caste, creed, race, or religion.
5. There would be joint electorates.
6. Services would go by merit alone.

7. Primary Education will be free and compulsory.
8. Every minority would have separate schools to train their children in their own tongue; their religious and cultural institutions would receive Government help also for these, but always in proportion to the taxes they pay into the common exchequer.
9. The residuary powers would be vested in the Central Government.
10. *Nagari* would be the national script, Hindi, the *lingua franca* and Sanskrit, the *Devabhasha* of India.

II

1. People would first of all welcome the machine age. The handicrafts would, of course, have their place and encouragement. But national production would be on the biggest possible machine scale.
2. As the peasantry and the working classes form literally the chief source of national wealth, health, and strength, every effort would be made to reinvigorate them and the villages which are their cradle. Peasants and labourers would be enabled to have their share in the distribution of wealth to such an extent as would enable them not only to live with a bare margin of existence, but with the average scale of a comfortable life, free from wants. Nevertheless, it would be remembered that they being a part and parcel of the nation as a whole, would share common obligations and responsibilities and therefore would only receive their share in such a way as would be consistent with the general development and security of national industry, manufacture and wealth in general.
3. As the national capital is under the present circumstances mainly individual and indispensable for the development of national industries and manufacturers, it would also receive due encouragement and recompense.
4. The interests of both the capital and labour would be subordinated to the requirements of the nation as a whole.

5. If an industry is flourishing, the profits would be shared in a large portion by the labourers. But on the contrary, if it is a losing concern, not only the capitalist, but to a certain extent even the labourers would have to remain satisfied with diminishing returns so that the National Industry as such would not altogether be undermined by the over bearing attitude of the selfish class interests of either the capitalists or the workers.
6. Every step would be taken by the State to protect national industries against foreign competition.
7. The key industries or manufactures and such other items would be altogether nationalised if the National Government could afford to do so and could conduct them more efficiently than private enterprise.
8. The same principle would apply to agriculture. Government would take over the land and introduce State cultivation if it could serve to train up the peasant class as a whole with the use of big machines and would cultivate on a large and scientific scale.
9. All strikes and lockouts which are obviously meant or inevitably tend to undermine and cripple national industries or production in general or are calculated to weaken the economic strength of the nation as a whole would be referred to State arbitration and settled, or in serious cases quelled.
10. Private property would be in general held inviolate. In no case there would be on the part of the State any expropriation of such property without reasonable recompense.

Thus Savarkar's India would be a democratic State in which the countrymen belonging to different religions, sects or races would be treated with perfect equality, and none would be allowed to dominate others or would be deprived of his just and equal rights of free citizenship, so long as every one discharges the common obligation which one owes to the State as a whole. Hindustan, the Motherland and Holyland of the Hindus, from the Indus to the Seas, would be an organic undivided State. The appellation of this Bharat Bhoomi would remain as Bharat or Hindustan.

In Savarkar's India, none would dare convert Hindus by fraud or force. Everywhere the Indians would be respected as citizens of a great nation. In that India, relative non-violence would be regarded as a virtue. The Hindus would be a casteless socket, a consolidated, modernised and up-to-date nation. Their marriage customs would be secularised and voluntary inter-caste marriages would be freely performed. Hindu corpses would be burnt in electric crematorium.

In Savarkar's India science would lead all material progress and annihilate superstitions. There would be a total liquidation of landlordism. All the land would belong to the State. All key industries would be nationalized. Agriculture would be mechanized. India would be self-sufficient in respect of food, clothes, shelter, and defence.

Savarkar's India would have unbounded faith in a World Commonwealth as his political philosophy conceives the Earth as the Common Motherland and humanism the patriotism of man, but his India would not go under during the process which leads to the welding of humanity into a World Commonwealth. In international politics Savarkar's India would help to build world peace and prosperity.

Savarkar's philosophy finds full expression in the Flag he has designed for the Hindus. It bears the symbol of *Kundalini* with the *Omkar* and *Kripan.*

Hindus have perfected the science of yoga. According to Savarkar, it is the highest blessing on human life; it is the contribution of the Hindus to mankind. This yoga means full development of man's internal powers. The symbol of that power is *Kundalini*. To attain the wonderfully supersensuous joy through the awakened *Kundalini* is, Savarkar opines, the highest ideal of man, be he a Hindu or a non-Hindu. In short, the *Kundalini* represents all the ultimate aspirations, feelings and powers of mankind. The *Kundalini* represents yoga, the highest spiritual attainment while the *Kripan* represents *Bhoga, Abhyudaya,* the worldly advancement. The red-orchard colour of the Flag indicates renunciation—*Tyaga*. And there is no renunciation without Yoga and *Kshama*—protection. Therefore the *Kripan* is for the Yoga *Kshama.*

The *Omkar* is the sacred symbol of the great One with Whom the liberated souls become one in the highest state of *Nihshreyas spiritual* bliss. It seems Savarkar was, with the exception of Aurobindo Ghose, the only first rate Indian leader who had experienced this supersensuous joy. He had practised this yoga while in the Cellular Jail of the Andamans. So Savarkar was the only political philosopher who chose *Kundalini* on the Flag. The Swastik was added to the Flag later on by the Hindu Mahasabha when it accepted the Flag. Originally it was not there.[1]

REFERENCE

1. Dhanajay Keer, *Veer Savarkar, op. cit.*, pp. 281-286.

BIBLIOGRAPHY

Aiyar, S.P. (ed.), *The Politics of Mass Violence in India* (Bombay: P.C. Manaktala & Sons), 1967.

Ambedkar, B.R., *Pakistan or The Partition of India* (Lahore: Mustafa Waheed), 1976.

Ambedkar, B.R., *What Congress and Gandhi have done to the Untouchables* (Bombay: Thacker & Co.), 1946.

Azad, Maulana Abul Kalam, *India Wins Freedom* (Madras: Orient Longman), 1989.

Bakshi, S.R., *Bhagat Singh, Patroit Martyr* (New Delhi: Anmol), 1990.

Bakshi, S.R., *V.D. Savarkar: Symbol of Sacrifice* (New Delhi: Anmol), 1994.

Bell Charles, *Indian Mutiny* (London: Clarendon Press), 1931.

Bimal Prasad (ed.), *A Revolutionary Quest* (Delhi: Oxford University Press), 1980.

Bose, S.K., *Tej Bahadur Sapru* (New Delhi: Publications Division, Ministry of Information & Broadcasting, Government of India), 1978.

Bose, Subhas Chandra, *The Indian Struggle* (Calcutta: Published for Netaji Publishing Society), 1948.

Chandra, Bipan, *Communalism in India* (New Delhi: Vani Educational Books), 1984.

Chandra, Bipan, *India's Struggle for Independence 1857-1947* (New Delhi: Viking), 1998.

Chandra, Bipan, *Modern India* (New Delhi: NCERT), 1976.

Chandra, Bipan, *Nationalism and Colonialism in Modern India* (New Delhi: Orient Longman), 1979.

Chaudhari, Sandhya, *Gandhi and Partition of India* (New Delhi: Sterling), 1984.

Chaudhary, Sukhbir, *Growth of Nationalism in India*, 2 Vols. (New Delhi: Trimurti Publications), 1973.

Chitkara, M.G., *Converts do not Make a Nation* (New Delhi: APH Publishing Company), 1998.

Chirol, Valentine, *The Indian Unrest* (New Delhi: Lights and Life Publications), 1979.

Chirol, Valentine, *India Old and New* (New Delhi: Lights and Life Publications), 1975.

Chitragupta, *Life of Barrister Savarkar* (Bombay: Veer Savarkar Prakashan), 1987.

Collins, Larry and Lapierre, Dominique, *Freedom at Midnight* (New Delhi: Vikas Publishing House), 1997.

Commemoration Volume on *Vinayak Damodar Savarkar* (Bombay: Savarkar Darshan Pratishthan), 1989.

Dalton, Dennis, *Indian Idea of Freedom* (New Delhi: Manohar), 1982.

Das, Durga, *India from Curzon to Nehru* (London: Collins), 1959.

Datta, V.N., *Madan Lal Dhingra and the Revolutionary Movement* (New Delhi: Vikas Publishing House), 1978.

Desai, A.R., *Social Background of Indian Nationalism* (Bombay: Popular Prakashan), 1976.

Dharamvira, *Lala Hardayal and Revolutionary Movements of His Times* (New Delhi: Indian Book Company), 1970.

Dignon, Don, *The Indian Revolutionary Problem in British Diplomacy 1914-1919* (New Delhi: Allied Publishers), 1983.

Dawarkadas, Kanji, *India's Fight for Freedom: An Eyewitness Story, 1913-37* (Bombay: Popular Prakashan), 1960.

Fawcett, C.B., *Frontiers—A Study in Political Geography* (London: OUP), 1921.

Gandhi, M.K., *An Autobiography or The Story of My Experiments with Truth* (Ahmedabad: Navajivan Publishing House), 1983.

Gandhi, M.K., *Hind Swaraj* (Ahmedabad: Navajivan Publishing House), 1983.

Ghosh, Kalicharan, *The Roll of Honours: Anecdotes of Indian Martyrs* (Calcutta: Vidya Baharati), 1975.

Ghokle, B.G., *Samudra Gupta: Life and Times* (Bombay Asia), 1962.

Gordan, A. Leonard, *Bengal: The Nationalist Movement, 1876-1940* (Delhi: Manohar), 1974.

Gordan, A. Leonard, *Brothers against the Raj* (New Delhi: Penguin Books), 1990.

Gooch, G. P., *Nationalism* (London: Longman), 1945.

Guha, A.C., *First Spark of Revolution* (Delhi: Orient Longman), 1972.

Hardayal, *Hints for Self Culture* (Delhi: Rajkamal Publications), 1948.

Hasan, Mushirul, *Nationalism and Communal Politics in India 1916-1928* (New Delhi: Manohar), 1981.

Hasan, Mushirul, *Communal Pan-Islamic Trends in Colonial India 1916-1928* (New Delhi: Manohar), 1981.

Holmes, T.R., *History of Indian Mutiny* (London: Macmillan), 1898.

Jayakar, M.R., *The Story of My Life*, 2 Volumes (Bombay: Asia Publishing House), 1958.

Jinnah, M.A., *Speeches and Writings* (Lahore: Mustaffa), 1960.

Jog, N.C., *Lokamanya Bal Gangadhar Tilak* (New Delhi: Publications Division, Ministry of Information & Broadcasting, Government of India), 1990.

Josh, Sohan Singh, *Hindustan Ghadar Party—A Short History* (New Delhi: People Publishing House), 1977.

Joshi, V.C., *Sri Aurobindo—An Interpretation* (New Delhi: Vikas Publishers), 1973.

Karan Singh, *Prophet of Indian Nationalism* (Bombay: Bharatiya Vidya Bhawan), 1991.

Karunakaran, K.P. (ed.), *Modern Indian Political Thought* (New Delhi: Allied Publishers), 1962.

Keer, Dhananjay, *Veer Savarkar* (Bombay: Popular Prakashan), 1966.

Ker, James Compbell, *Political Trouble in India* (Calcutta: Superintendent Government Printing), 1917.

Laski, Harold, *Grammar of Politics* (London: Allen), 1948.

Malleson, G.B. and Kye John, *History of Indian Mutiny* (London: Allen), 1879.

Masani, R.P., *Dadabhai Naoroji* (New Delhi: Publications Division, Ministry of Information & Broadcasting, Government of India), 1960.

Masselos, Jim, *Indian Nationalism: A History* (New Delhi: Sterling), 1985.

Mathur, L.P., *Indian Revolutionary Movement in USA* (Delhi: S. Chand), 1970.

Mazumdar, R.C., Roy Chaudhary, H.C. Dutta, Kali Kumar, *An Advanced History of India* (Madras: Macmillan), 1950.

Mazumdar, S.N., *In Search of a Revolutionary Ideology* (New Delhi: People Publishing House), 1979.

McCarthy, Justin, *History of Our Times*, Vol. II (London: Chatts), 1897.

Mead, Henery, *The Sepoy Revolt: Its Causes & Consequences* (Delhi: Gyan), 1986.

Mody, Homi, *Pherozeshah Mehta* (New Delhi: Publications Division, Ministry of Information & Broadcasting, Government of India), 1963.

Nanda, B.R., *Gandhi, Pan-Islamism, Imperialism and Nationalism in India* (Bombay: Oxford University Press), 1989.

Nath, Shaileshwar, *Terrorism in India* (New Delhi: National Publishing House), 1980.

Nehru, Jawaharlal, *An Autobiography* (London: The Bodley Head), 1958.

Noorani, A.G., *Savarkar and Hindutva* (New Delhi: Left Word), 2002.

Parmanand, Bhai, *The Story of My Life* (New Delhi: S. Chand), 1982.

Parekh, Bhikhu, *Colonialism, Tradition and Reform* (Delhi: Sage Publications), 1999.

Philips, C.H. (ed.), *The Evolution of India and Pakistan 1858-1947 Select Documents* (London: George Allen & Unwin), 1962.

Radhakrishnan, S. (ed.), *Mahatma Gandhi* (London: George Allen), 1949.

Rai, Lala Lajpat, The *Story of My Life* (New Delhi: D.A.V. Publications), 1987.

Rai, Lala Lajpat, *Young India: An Interpretation and a History of the Nationalist Movement from Within* (New Delhi: Publications Division, Ministry of Information & Broadcasting, Government of India), 1968.

Rajendra Prasad, *An Autobiography* (Bombay: Asia Publishing House), 1957.

Ralhan, O.P. (ed.), *Hindu Mahasabha*, 2 Vols. (New Delhi: Anmol), 1997.

Ray, Sibnarayan (ed.), *M.N. Roy, Philosopher and Revolutionary* (Delhi: Oxford University Press), 1987.

Reddy, P.L. Sanjeev and Mishra, S.N. (eds.), *Sardar Vallabhbhai Patel: The Nation Builder* (New Delhi: Indian Institute of Public Administration), 2004.

Rolland Romain, *The Life of Vivekananda and the Universal Gospel* (Calcutta: Advaita Ashrama), 1953.

Sarojini, Naidu, *Speeches and Writings* (Madras: G.A. Natesan), 1945.

Savarkar, V.D., *Hindu-Pad-Padshahi* (Pune: Kelkar), 1925.

Savarkar, V.D., *Hindu Rashtra Darshan* (Bombay: Veer Savarkar Prakashan), 1984.

Savarkar, V.D., *Hindutva: Who is a Hindu*? (Bombay: Veer Savarkar Prakashan), 1969.

Savarkar, V.D., *Six Glorious Epics in Indian History* (New Delhi: Rajdhani Granthagar), 1970.

Savarkar, V.D., *Swantantryaveer Savarkar: A Guide to Indian Revolutionary Movement* (Pune: Maharashtra Prantik Hindu Sabha), 1963.

Savarkar, V.D., *The Indian War of Independence 1847* (New Delhi: Phoenix), 1947.

Savarkar, V.D., *The Story of My Transportation of Life* (Bombay: Sadbhakti Publications), 1950.

Savarkar, V.D., *Echo from Andamans* (Poona: Venus Books), 1947.

Savarkar, S.S. & Joshi G.M., *Historic Statements of V.D. Savarkar*, (Bombay: Popular Prakashan), 1967.

Shankar, Ramahari, *Gandhi's Encounter with Indian Revolutionaries* (New Delhi: Siddharth Publications), 1996.

Shankhdher, M.M., *Reflections on Indian Politics* (New Delhi: Kumar Brothers), 1973.

Sharma, Jai Narain, *Power, Politics & Corruption: A Gandhian Solution* (New Delhi: Deep and Deep), 2004.

Sharma, Malikarjuna, *Role of Revolutionaries in the Freedom Struggle* (Hyderabad: Marxist Study Forum), 1987.

Sharma Rashmi (ed.), *Sonia* versus *Vajpayee* (New Delhi: Deep and Deep), 2004.

Shraddhanand, Swami, *Inside Congress* (Bombay: Phoenix), 1946.

Singh, Gulab, *Under the Shadow of Gallows*: A *Story of a Revolutionary* (Delhi: Rup Chand), 1964.

Singhal, Jwala Prasad, *Sphinx Speaks: The Story of Pre-historic Nations* (New Delhi: Sadgya), 1963.

Sitaramayya, Pattabhi, *History of Indian National Congress* (Delhi: S. Chand & Co.), 1969.

Srivastava, Harindra, *Five Stormy Years: Savarkar in London* (New Delhi: Allied Publishers), 1983.

Suda, J.P., *Main Currents of Social and Political Thought in India*, Vol. III (Meerut: K. Nath & Co.), 1973.

Sullivan, O. Noel (ed.), *Terrorism, Ideology and Revolution* (Sussex: The Harvester Press), 1986.

Tara Chand, *History of Freedom Movement in India* (New Delhi: Publications Division, Ministry of Information & Broadcasting, Government of India), 1962.

Tendulkar, D.G., *Mahatma*, 8 Vols. (New Delhi: Publications Division, Ministry of Information & Broadcasting, Government of India), 1958.

The Complete Works of Swami Vivekananda (Calcutta: Advaita Ashrama), 1994.

Trehan, Jyoti, *Veer Savarkar* (New Delhi: Deep and Deep), 1991.

Varma, V.P., *Modern Indian Political Thought* (Agra: Luxmi Narain Agarwal), 1961.

Vajpeyi, J.N., *The Extremist Movement in India* (Allahabad: Chug Publications), 1974.

Wardlow, Grant, *Political Terrorism Theory, Tactics and Counter Measures* (Cambridge: Cambridge University Press), 1982.

Walport, Stanley, *Jinnah of Pakistan* (New Delhi: Oxford University Press), 1965.

Walport, Stanley, *Tilak & Gokhale* (Bombay: University of California Press), 1962.

Wilkinson, Paul, *Political Terrorism* (New York: Macmillan), 1976.

Wasti, Syed Razi, *Lord Minto and the Indian National Movement 1905-1910* (London: Oxford University Press), 1965.

Zangwill, Israel, *Principles of Nationalities* (London: Heinemann), 1920.

Index